GAINING
GROUND
with Good Soil

Learning to Share God's Redemptive Story in a
World of Competing Faiths and Cultures

By Gil Thomas

www.GoodSoil.com

Published by

Good Soil Evangelism and Discipleship

ISBN: 978-1-888796-79-7

Library of Congress Cataloging-in-Publications Data (application pending)

Printed in The United States of America.

Gaining Ground with Good Soil
Learning to Share God's Redemptive Story in a World of Competing Faiths and Cultures

Cover Design and Artwork: Miriam Miller Design
Interior Design: Miriam Miller Design
Custom Photography: Jeff Raymond
Stock Photography: 123rf.com

Author: Thomas, Gilbert H. (1959–)

Email: Info@GoodSoil.com
Web: www.GoodSoil.com
Order: 1.877.959.2293

This book is dedicated to my dear wife, Denise.
After the Lord Jesus Christ,
no one has helped me *gain ground*
in all areas of my life more than she.

When it comes to ways of thinking and communicating, people live in decidedly different worlds. People of our Western world, for example, tend to think and speak propositionally and conceptually and give priority to linear, sequential reasoning and analysis. People in much of the non-Western world, on the other hand, tend to think and speak pictorially, giving preference to stories, parables, aphorisms, and concrete relationships.

… Good Soil strategy represents the best of both worlds! Gil Thomas has effectively communicated that Good Soil strategy in his easy-to-read narrative.

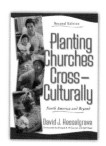

(from the Foreword by)
David J. Hesselgrave
Professor Emeritus of Missions
Trinity Evangelical Divinity School
Author of many books, including *Planting Churches Cross-Culturally*

Gaining Ground with Good Soil just may not only challenge your present approach to sharing the gospel, but change it! It just may help move the recipients of the good news that you presented beyond understanding and embracing, to retaining it. Gil Thomas presents a story with substance that you don't want to overlook.

Tom Steffen
Cook School of Intercultural Studies, Biola University
Author of several books, including *Passing the Baton*

Gaining Ground with Good Soil brings a practical method for anyone seeking to make evangelism and discipleship more effective in his or her field of ministry. Post-literate America needs to know the truth seeds of Scripture delivered in a way that stimulates growth. Gil Thomas' years of mission experience give us a sharpened tool to plow wisely through the crust and dig deep into the heart where truth can transform a life. I am recommending this to our leadership team.

Paul Krueger
Director of Discipling Oral Learners, a ministry of The Navigators

Gaining Ground with Good Soil effectively addresses the challenge of making the Gospel of Christ understandable by presenting an insightful and adaptable model using narrative and exercises to teach effective church-planting principles and practices on a worldview level. Field application of the principles presented in this book will help users know that host societies were able to make *good soil* decisions about God's Word, specifically the Gospel of Christ.

Mark Zook
New Tribes Missionary featured in *Ee-Taow! The Mouk Story*
Co-Founder of Worldview Resource Group

We can no longer assume that the unchurched of North America under-stand, or are even acquainted with, the foundational concepts of the gospel. They don't understand who the true God is, what sin is and how it impacts their lives, and who Jesus Christ is and what He has done for them. The Good Soil Evangelism and Discipleship training seminars developed by the Asso-ciation of Baptists for World Evangelism (ABWE) equip Christ-followers to communicate the essential elements of the gospel thoroughly and clearly to adherents of any worldview, regardless of their gospel knowledge defi-ciencies. Gil Thomas has embedded the essence of that worldview-relevant evangelism and discipleship training in this clever and interesting narrative—*Gaining Ground with Good Soil*.

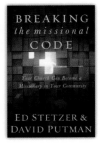

Ed Stetzer
President of LifeWay Research
Author of many books, including *Breaking the Missional Code*

Acknowledgments

I read somewhere that a book is a joint effort. I have found this to be true. I am amazed at all the people who contributed unselfishly to make this book a reality.

In 1986, Denise and I went to Portugal to serve God as church-planting missionaries with the Association of Baptists for World Evangelism (ABWE). We worked twenty-three years with the International Ministry Team there, which we had the privilege of leading for twelve of those years. Thanks, Team, for being used of God to develop me as a leader and minister of the gospel. In 2004, a team of missionaries was invited by Dr. Loftis, ABWE's president, to develop training programs for missionaries in the areas of evangelism, discipleship, Bible teaching, and church planting. The Core Ministries Institute Team was formed soon afterward. Some good work was begun on the Good Soil project by this team.

Thanks, CMI, for stretching me as I participated in this training team.

In 2008, I was invited to lead the Good Soil E&D project out of ABWE's home office in Harrisburg, Pennsylvania. By then, Wayne Haston, Ron Berrus, and Dave Southwell had developed the Good Soil Evangelism and Discipleship Seminar along with some other key teachers.

As I took on my new role, I believed a narrative could be written to communicate the Good Soil principles to a wider audience. Thanks, guys, for allowing me to take your work and put it into this book.

The Thomas Family In Portugal

Others have read the manuscript and offered excellent editing advice. Then several readers from all walks of life were chosen to read and offer their critiques on the final draft. Thanks to all of you who invested time and effort to critique the book. Miriam Miller and Wayne Haston put in many hours to make this second edition so appealing. The second edition is far better because of you two. Thank you so much.

THE THOMASES IN PORTUGAL

Table of Contents

Foreword

When it comes to ways of thinking and communicating, people live in decidedly different worlds. People of our Western world, for example, tend to think and speak propositionally and conceptually and give priority to linear, sequential reasoning and analysis. People in much of the non-Western world, on the other hand, tend to think and speak pictorially, giving preference to stories, parables, aphorisms, and concrete relationships.

> *People in much of the non-Western world tend to think and speak pictorially, giving preference to stories, parables, aphorisms, and concrete relationships.*

The Mediterranean world of the first century was much the same. Accordingly, the Lord Jesus tended to communicate "concretely" by employing pictures and parables. Paul, on the other hand, tended to communicate "conceptually," in terms of propositions and precepts. In a profound sense, therefore, Jesus and the apostles "contextualized" the gospel. They spoke and wrote, not to one thought world, but to at least two thought worlds (and probably more)!

In our twenty-first century globalized world, geographical boundaries are crossed easily and routinely, but differing "thought worlds" are not so easily penetrated. Contextualization is just as important now as it was two thousand years ago—perhaps more so. And precisely that is the beauty and blessing of ABWE's "Good Soil" approach and program to missionizing. Very wisely, ABWE leaders have not only contextualized the gospel, they have also contextualized church and mission. And in so doing they have not only retained the unchanging truth of biblical revelation, they have also incorporated the accumulated knowledge that stems from long experience and careful research.

Any way you look at it, ABWE's "Good Soil" strategy represents the best of both worlds! Gil Thomas has effectively communicated that Good Soil strategy in his easy-to-read narrative.

David J. Hesselgrave
Professor Emeritus of Missions
Trinity Evangelical Divinity School
Author of many books, including *Planting Churches Cross-Culturally*

Preface

This book is intended to be ***interactively instructional***. My desire is to communicate vital principles in an enjoyable narrative form while giving you opportunities to stop and grapple with truths through written exercises along the way. That said, I would like to address three subjects relative to your enjoyment and learning.

Setting

The setting is Germany and Portugal. It has been said, "A movie should take you somewhere." I believe a book should do the same. So our heroes are missionaries and the international leaders with whom they work throughout Europe. That doesn't mean this book is not for you if you don't live in Europe. On the contrary, the principles in this book are cross-cultural and multinational in scope.

Language

People who live in another culture, speak more than one language, and/or work with internationals, often let a word or two from their second (or third!) language slip into their conversations. It's natural. The people to whom they are speaking don't miss a beat because they know both languages, too. Often the word that "slipped into" the conversation communicates the idea better for both speaker and hearer. In fact, that word usually carries more meaning for them at the time—otherwise they would not have used it.

I have allowed that to happen in some of the conversations in this book. I enjoy learning words from other languages as I interact with people, watch movies, or when I am reading books. I know others who also do. However, I realize some people *do not* enjoy it. For some it may be frustrating, even irritating, because they don't know how to pronounce the words and feel they can't even guess at the meaning. If you are in that category, please realize the following:

> *Having the foreign words included makes the narrative more realistic. Including some foreign words in context helps put you in another country and culture. It may help you feel what it is like to be in the speaker's shoes.*
>
> *It might be more enjoyable than you realize. Try to pronounce*

the words. Try to guess what they mean by the context. When it is too hard to guess, I've included the meaning in the margin or in parentheses.

Exercises

Please do the exercises. It may be *easier* to skip over an exercise and keep following the story, but if you do, you will not *learn* nearly as much. When you come to an exercise, stop. Think through the task. Open your Bible if asked and read the passage. Write your answer(s) in the space provided. You will gain much more if you do. An individual study guide and a leader's guide for group study are also available.

The purpose of Good Soil Evangelism and Discipleship is to motivate, train, and resource people in worldview-relevant evangelism. If you want to know more, visit www.GoodSoil.com or write to Info@GoodSoil.com.

Interactive exercises will be marked by this icon.

Free Instructional Resources

Individual Study Guide

A free guide for personal study of *Gaining Ground with Good Soil*. Ideal resource for those who are not able to attend a Good Soil seminar, but who want to gain optimal benefit from reading the book.

Leader's Guide

A free instructor's guide for leading a group of participants through *Gaining Ground with Good Soil*. Includes a wide variety of creative and interactive teaching methods. Great for Sunday school classes or small group Bible studies.

PowerPoint Presentation

A free PowerPoint presentation to be used in conjunction with the *Gaining Ground with Good Soil* Leader's Guide. Contains professionally designed slides.

Supplemental Teaching Resources

A free set of teaching resources to be used in conjunction with the Leader's Guide for *Gaining Ground with Good Soil*. Resources designed to make class learning more enjoyable and more effective.

Free download at: www.GoodSoil.com/Free

Breaking the News

"We will be leaving Germany in June, and we'd like to use the next six months as a transition for you two to take over the ministry here," Greg Tillman burst out. He could hardly believe he had said it. He and Diana had talked and prayed about this subject enough, but now, as they sat with their German colleagues staring back at them in disbelief, it was hard to believe the words had come out of his mouth.

But this is the right thing to do, isn't it? For nine and a half years now—*after* two years of language study—he and Diana had been trying to start a church in Frankfurt, Germany, a city of 1.8 million people, with only a handful of believers to show for their efforts. Now he and Diana believed they must have been mistaken about God's leading them there in the first place. That's why they planned this four-day retreat with Bernard and Miriam Sämann to inform them of their decision, to see if they could get them to continue the tiny work they had started, and to plan some kind of transition. At least then they wouldn't feel as if they were total failures!

Miriam spoke first, a big tear rolling down her cheek. "No, you can't go!" was all she could get out before bursting into tears and covering her face in her hands. Diana slid across the couch, put her arm around Miriam, and sobbed quietly with her. This was not easy.

Bern and Miri were the last people they wanted to leave or to hurt. Ever since they graduated from seminary and joined Greg and Di three years ago, their hearts had been knit together like neither couple had experienced before.

Bernard took a deep breath and let it out slowly. He stood, walked to the window, and looked out at the huge white dome covering the maze of blue and green water slides.

The two families had come to Monte Mare in Kaiserslautern for a getaway and were staying in an aparthotel. The kids were having fun swimming and sliding inside the warm dome as snow fell on this dreary January morning. Bernard was thinking it had just gotten drearier. Had the clouds thickened? Or was it just this news falling down on the room like a heavy blanket, darkening their future? As he prayed a quick "Why, God?" and "Help us figure this out," the blanket seemed to lift a little.

Germany

- Hamburg
- Hanover
- Berlin
- Frankfurt
- ★ Kaiserslautern
- Munich

Aparthotel:
a hotel made up
of apartments
instead of rooms

"Wait!" Bernard blurted out. "Just—hold on." His pause seemed to last for minutes, but in reality, just a few seconds later he added, "I'm sure you have been thinking and praying about this for some time, and I respect that. But will you wait until the retreat is over before you decide?"

Greg countered, "I know it's difficult. We love you guys and hate to think about being so far apart, and our kids and your kids ..." With his heart in his throat, Greg was having difficulty speaking. "But, like we said, we're not seeing fruit. I'm just not sure we were cut out for this kind of thing. God doesn't seem to be using us."

"But you know that Germany—all of Western Europe—is unresponsive," Miriam ventured as she lifted up her head to speak.

"But you know that Germany—all of Western Europe—is unresponsive," Miriam ventured as she lifted up her head to speak.

"Yes, but ... ," Bernard interrupted Greg. "Listen for just a second," he managed before taking another deliberate, deep breath. "If you can just wait four more days to decide, we'll stand behind your decision and pray seriously about caring for the work by ourselves.

"You see, I've been noticing something recently in my study of one of Jesus' parables, and I think it relates to what we are talking about. I wonder if we are even going about evangelism as we should. I think if we all study what Jesus said and work together on this ..."

"And pray," interrupted Miriam.

"... and pray." Bernard smiled. "We may come up with a better model. Could we spend the next few days in Bible study and prayer and *then* make a decision? We've already set aside the time."

"And we're already here," Diana interjected.

Miriam, buoyed with hope at this possibility, added, "And you always say, Greg, that 'you can't get enough of the Word ...'"

"... as long as you're applying it!" they all finished one of Greg's favorite sayings in unison.

"Well, we certainly have nothing to lose by spending some time in the Word, seeking God's face together. What do you say we pray now, then join the kids on the slides, and come back together after lunch?" Greg asked.

With that, the four friends prayed as earnestly as they ever had that God would teach them during these next few days, that they would gain an understanding of evangelism as Jesus taught, and even that God would work in a special way to keep Greg and Diana in Germany.

Refreshed and encouraged, the two couples hugged one another, then left to find their swimsuits and their kids.

Part One

HELPING *US*
UNDERSTAND
the Gospel

What Is "Good Soil"?
Dealing with the Passages

After lunch, Diana settled their girls, Kaylie (9) and Julie (6), in their suite for an afternoon of board games while little Allie (10 months) napped. The Sämanns had already dropped off their boys, Gustav (12) and Misha (8), and headed down the hall with Greg, Bibles and notepads in hand. Amber, Greg's twenty-two year old sister, was in Germany for four months to help the Tillmans with their children and experience a bit of what it is like to live in another country and culture. She watched both sets of children while the couples met together.

"Okay, there are snacks on the counter," Diana told the kids. "Be good and obey Amber." Then, addressing Amber, she added, "If you need anything, we will be in the lounge overlooking the lobby."

Diana was confused but happy. She and Greg had dreaded this retreat because they did not want to tell the Sämann family they were leaving. They really didn't want to leave Germany—whose people they had come to love—but they just were not getting anywhere, and they didn't know what to do to change that. Was this merely postponing the inevitable, making the final decision even harder? Or was there something they were missing … something that could make a substantial difference in making disciples here? Well, the decision was made to spend the time in the Word. So, at least for a few days she could just enjoy fellowship around the Word and see what God might do. Maybe they wouldn't have to leave. Wouldn't that be great? Diana was caught between a desperate desire to hope and the dread of having to go through the pain of decision making all over again.

> *They really didn't want to leave Germany … but they just were not getting anywhere, and they didn't know what to do to change that.*

Please work in our hearts and minds, God, she thought as she approached the team. *Enlighten us with Your Word.* "Where do we start, Bern?" she asked, holding up her Bible.

"Okay. Now, as I said, I've been studying one of the parables and its parallel passages, but I don't necessarily have any conclusive answers," Bernard started to say as Diana sat down opposite him. They were all seated in

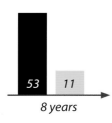

comfortable chairs in a cozy setting, Bibles and notepads in front of them on the coffee table. "But I've noticed something that I think could be significant as it relates to really reaching people with the message of Christ."

"Great, let's take a look," replied Greg, and the women nodded their assent. Diana peered closely at Greg. Was he being genuine or just not wanting to disappoint the others? He always hated to disappoint people.

"And I think we all need to participate actively to get the most from our study," Bernard continued.

"Greg wouldn't have it any other way!" Diana teased lightly as she winked at her husband. Greg was an excellent Bible teacher who emphasized the need for interaction in all his teaching. He often said the best way to learn was to be involved: "head, hands, heart, and tongue."

Greg smiled back, but cleared his throat, and took on a more serious tone as he said, "Well, if something is really going to be learned—if it is going to go from short-term memory to long-term memory—you have to …"

"… interact with the material at least six times!" they all finished.

"Well, at least something is getting through." Greg sighed as he held up his Bible to Bernard in a plea to let them know where to turn.

Bible References:
Matthew 13:23
Mark 4:20
Luke 8:15

"Matthew 13:23 for you, Greg, Mark 4:20 for you, Di, and Miri, open to Luke 8:15," Bernard responded. "But first, let's make sure we're all coming from the same direction."

"Am I right in saying that the problem, as we see it here, is that we have not seen a church take root in Frankfurt after several years of work? Sunday mornings we only have eleven believers meeting with us—on a good day— right?"

The group nodded their agreement, wishing it were not so.

"Now," Bernard continued, "it's true that evangelism is said to be slow here in my native land of Germany, so we shouldn't be surprised if large numbers of people have not become believers. But the truth of the matter is that, according to the figures I checked this morning, during the past eight years fifty-three people have 'prayed the sinner's prayer' as some would say. My question to consider before we look at the Bible texts is this: *Why are those people not now part of our group, living the kind of life that identifies them as followers of Jesus Christ?* Think about that and write your answer on your notepad."

| 53 | 11 |

8 years

After the group had worked silently for a few minutes Greg was the first to respond. "I wonder if the people who prayed really didn't understand what they were doing or even the whole gospel message."

"How about lack of follow-up?" Miriam piped up. "Sometimes, whether it was our fault or theirs, we just haven't helped people grow after their decisions."

"A lot of times they don't want help," Greg responded, maybe a bit too defensively. "Remember, I went to have a Bible study with Dietrich, and he practically threw me off his doorstep! And that was after he had prayed to receive Christ as Savior! That wasn't very Christlike."

"No, it wasn't, but maybe there was something else going on with him we haven't figured out yet," replied Bernard. "Let's not lose sight of any of these examples, but for now, let's keep going. So far we have 'lack of follow-up' and 'didn't really understand,'" he said slowly as he wrote them on the foldout flip chart they had brought along.

"What I wrote on my paper really has two sides to it," Bernard continued. "Here's the idea: People either say 'yes' or—you know—they make a decision, to get us off their backs or to please us. One is kind of positive, and the other is negative, but we really don't want either response."

"Yes, I know what you mean," Diana said. "Last month Berte prayed with me, and I was surprised. I really didn't think she was ready, but she prayed. However, since then I can't get her to return my calls."

"Many times we don't have that problem because we Germans like to say it the way it is," admitted Miriam. "But some of us *are* sweet."

"And I married one of them," Bernard jumped right in, not passing up an opportunity like that.

Miriam blushed and, trying to divert the attention away from her, asked, "How about you, Diana? What did you write down?"

"I had a hard time with this, but I wrote something maybe you'll think is silly. I put: 'The soil was not prepared,'" Diana answered.

> Why are those people not now part of our group, living the kind of life that identifies them as followers of Jesus Christ?
>
> - Didn't Understand
> - Lack of Follow-Up
> - Said "yes" to please or get us off their backs
> - Soil was not prepared

Exercise #1:

Can you think of any other possible reasons people may make a profession of faith but don't seem to become part of a local church?

The group's possible reasons:
- Didn't Understand
- Lack of Follow-Up
- Said "yes" to please or get us off their backs
- Soil was not prepared

Your additional possible reasons:

-

-

-

-

"Wow! That's not silly at all. That may be the best answer theologically we have heard yet!" said Greg proudly. "That's my girl."

"*Jah*, from which seminary did you say she got her doctorate?" Bernard chided. "That's an insightful answer, and it comes from the passages I wanted to study, so why don't we do that now?"

Ripping off three sheets from the flip chart, Bernard asked the group to read the assigned passages and copy their verses onto the large sheet of paper he had given them. After writing out the verses, they taped each paper on the wall so they all could look at the passages at the same time. Then Bernard asked the women to scrutinize the verses and write down how the passages were different. He added that he and Greg would write down how they were similar.

> **Matthew 13:23**
> As for what was sown on good soil, this is the one who hears the word and understands it. He indeed bears fruit and yields, in one case a hundredfold, in another sixty, and in another thirty.

> **Mark 4:20**
> But those that were sown on the good soil are the ones who hear the word and accept it and bear fruit, thirtyfold and sixtyfold and a hundredfold.

> **Luke 8:15**
> As for that in the good soil, they are those who, hearing the word, hold it fast in an honest and good heart, and bear fruit with patience.

How are these accounts similar?

How are these accounts different?

Exercise #2:

Use the space provided to make your own observations about how the verses are similar or different.

Diana and Miriam finished their observations before the men, so Diana ran down the hall to check on Amber and the kids. They were doing fine, about halfway through a Monopoly® game. But how can one judge "halfway" with Monopoly®? Little Julie, the youngest of the four, was winning so far. Little Allie, still waking up from her nap, was sitting contentedly in Amber's lap.

Diana brought back some soft drinks and peanuts just as the guys finished up.

"Okay, we'll report first," Greg said. "The versions of the parable are quite similar. We saw that in each passage the Word was heard, which is the seed that was sown. It produced a crop of some kind, and *good soil* was mentioned."

"You guys did a good job with the similarities, Greg," encouraged Diana as she began their report. "We were looking for the differences in the passages. First of all, we noticed that the words describing the response of the *good soil* hearer, as the Matthew passage calls him, are different in each of the passages. In Matthew, the *good soil* hearer *understands* the word, while those who hear (plural in the other two passages) in Mark and Luke *accept* it and *hold it fast*, respectively."

"Interesting," interrupted Greg. "I never noticed that before."

"Yes, it is fascinating," answered Miriam. "We were wondering if they are actually different words in the original or not. That could be significant."

"Indeed, it could, Miri," said Bernard. "Indeed, it could. I'd like to share what I discovered about that in a minute. But first, did you find anything else?"

"Well," interjected Diana, "we also noticed that the actual harvest was explained differently in the passages. Matthew and Mark speak of the seed producing one hundred, sixty and thirty—in opposite orders, by the way." Diana did a mock curtsy as she commented.

"Oh, very observant," interrupted Greg.

"And Luke also gives a greater description of those who are *good soil*, speaking of 'those with a noble and good heart,'" finished Diana with a wave of her hand and another bow.

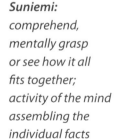

Suniemi: comprehend, mentally grasp or see how it all fits together; activity of the mind assembling the individual facts into an organized whole

"Great! You picked out some good differences," applauded Bernard. "It was exactly the different words the Gospel writers used for the response that caught my eye a couple of weeks ago, so I began looking up the original words. They are different. And I think it is significant. Let me write them on our study chart as I share them.

"In Matthew, the Greek word for understands is *suniemi*. It has the idea of getting your arms all the way around something—to have it all with you. It is

a complete, comprehensive understanding. According to Matthew, the one who received the seed that fell on *good soil* gets it. He is one who really understands. He has a handle on it—there is no doubt about it. It's kind of like putting the pieces of a puzzle all together to see the big picture."

According to Matthew, the one who received the seed that fell on good soil gets it.

Miriam asked, "So some of the fifty-three people who *made decisions* may not have *gotten it*?"

"Aha. Good insight, Miri. It may very well be that they made a quasi decision without a true understanding," Greg interjected.

"Thus, a lack of commitment," added Diana.

"*Jah*, that's possible, but of course we don't know. What we do know is that we probably need more *good soil* decisions, and one of the ways to get those is to be sure our hearers 'get it'; that they really understand the gospel. This probably ought to be one of the areas we work on during the next three days, but for now, let's look at the other two words describing the response.

Paradechomai: receive with open arms, welcome, or embrace; to acknowledge as one's own

"Mark says the ones who hear the word and accept it are those who produce fruit. The word is a biggie: *paradechomai*, which means to receive with open arms, welcome, or embrace. It is the same word used in Luke 15 where the Pharisees said that Jesus *welcomes* sinners and eats with them. You could almost see Jesus' eyes light up with that description—after all, that *was* His purpose—receiving sinners. But the Pharisees saw a problem with it. While Jesus embraced sinners in love, welcoming them to His family, the Pharisees wanted to push them away."

"So the Mark passage says the hearer is one who acknowledges the gospel as his very own; he embraces it; he wants it," Greg ventured. He was really getting into this now.

"Well put, partner," cheered Bernard. Then he continued. "Now the word in Luke, *katecho* means to hold it fast, retain, or hang onto as you would something you did not want to lose; refuse to let go. Notice that these people will persevere. The text says that they 'hold it fast, and bear fruit with patience.'"

Katecho: hold it fast, retain, hold firmly so that something will not be snatched away

"Hmm, three passages, three different words with different meanings," Greg thought out loud, "and they all have to do with *positive* responses to the gospel."

"The ones where the seed was sown on *good soil*," added Diana.

"So what we want are, well, *good soil* responses," ventured Miriam.

"But according to the parable, won't there always be some seed falling on other soils?" asked Diana.

> *"I'm wondering if we can contribute to more good soil responses if we comprehend these words of Jesus better and work harder at making sure our hearers understand, embrace, and retain the gospel."*

"Looks like it," answered Greg. "But I think we ought to be working toward more *good soil* decisions. I'm wondering, and I think this is where Bernard was hoping we'd arrive, if we can contribute to more *good soil* responses by comprehending these words of Jesus better and working harder at making sure our hearers *understand*, *embrace*, and *retain* the gospel. I can just about guarantee that the majority of those fifty-three decisions we recorded over the past years have not understood, embraced, and evidently not retained the good news. Can we change what we're doing in some way to cultivate more *good soil* decisions?"

"And therefore, fruit that remains!" Di and Miri said almost in unison. Everyone looked at each other in wide-eyed surprise and then burst out laughing. The tension from the first hour was past. An energy they had not felt for who knows how long had once again permeated the group. It was almost like those first months, a decade ago, when they had such strong hopes for making an impact for Christ. None of them knew where this was going to lead, but they all felt a fresh look at this parable held something dynamic, something crucial for making—what were they calling it now?—"Good Soil Disciples."

They were all enjoying the study and fellowship so much they had not noticed the hour. Just then, Allie, hands on her stomach, approached the foursome with Amber and the rest of the kids trailing. "Hungy, Mommy," she blurted out.

"You know what? I am, too!" said Diana, picking up her youngest and giving her a squeeze. "What do you say we stop for now, and I help Aunt Miri make her famous *Wienersnitzel* we were planning for supper?"

"Yummy!" shouted the little one, her face illumined by a smile of delight.

"I'll need a couple of things from the store," commented Miriam.

"Bernard and I have got it covered," Greg answered. "But before we go, let me just say this has been great. Whether it makes any difference for our future or not remains to be seen, but it is fun anyway. After we eat, let's have a prayer time and start back at this in the morning."

After brief affirmative answers from everyone (including an especially enthusiastic one from the youngster), the women went to make supper and the men bundled up the kids and went to the store.

The snow was falling lightly, giving the earth a clean, white blanket. Greg sucked in the sharp, cold air as he thought back over the discussion of the last several hours. It was not what he had expected, but he was encouraged. The snow seemed to be symbolic of the new thought patterns developing in his mind. Could they be onto something that could change their ministry and keep them in Germany? He breathed a prayer of thanks and turned his attention to the kids. "Who wants to have a snowball fight after supper?"

By the end of their time together that afternoon, their notes looked like this.

Matthew 13:23
As for what was sown on good soil, this is the one who hears the word and understands it. He indeed bears fruit and yields, in one case a hundredfold, in another sixty, and in another thirty.

Mark 4:20
But those that were sown on the good soil are the ones who hear the word and accept it and bear fruit, thirtyfold and sixtyfold and a hundredfold.

Luke 8:15
As for that in the good soil, they are those who, hearing the word, hold it fast in an honest and good heart, and bear fruit with patience.

Similarities:
- Hear word
- Produce crop
- Good Soil
- Seed same in all
- "it" = the Word

Differences:
- Different words for response
- Harvest explained differently
- Noble & good heart— greater description
- Singular/Plural

Where Do the Seeds Fall?
Relating Our Study to Engel's Scale

Greg opened his eyes, surprised. He had just slept through the night—something that hadn't happened for quite some time. He felt rested, invigorated. After thoroughly enjoying Miri's homemade *Wienersnitzel*, he and Bernard "lost" a fierce snowball fight to the kids and served the winners hot cocoa. Then they tucked the kids into bed and had a wonderful prayer time with their colleagues. This morning they were going to get back to their study/strategy. Greg was eagerly anticipating this, more than he had anticipated anything in a long time.

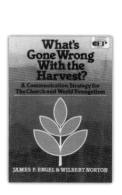

"Hey, sleepyhead, rise and shine!" called Diana. "How about breakfast? Say, in ten minutes?"

Greg bounded out of bed and into the bathroom. "You don't have to call me twice!" he shouted as he turned on the water.

After breakfast and family Bible reading and prayer time, the kids were in their swimsuits again and off to the slides with Amber. The Tillman and Sämann couples brought their Bibles and notepads to the lobby overlooking the vast pool area so they could keep track of the kids as they worked. Bern toted his laptop as well.

Bern recapped the former day's work: "We've discovered that people characterized as being *good soil* in Jesus' parable understand, embrace, and retain the good news that they have heard."

"Right. So how can we ensure that people understand, embrace, and retain the gospel? What should we be doing differently?" Diana asked. "We proclaim the gospel, right? But is ours a task of persuading people as well? Isn't persuading really the Holy Spirit's job?"

"Hmm. Proclaim. Persuade." It was Greg who had spoken, but he sat thinking so long that the others weren't sure he was going to continue. Just when Diana was about to say something, he continued. "I read a book in seminary titled *What's Gone Wrong with the Harvest?* by Engel and Norton. And you'll never believe this: I dug it out and dusted it off recently because we were struggling so with the harvest here in Germany. I even stuffed it in my suitcase and brought it with me to Monte Mare. Anyway, James Engel

> ### *We are to proclaim the gospel as a somewhat general task, then persuade specific unbelievers, and then cultivate believers.*

used those two terms, proclaim and persuade, in a way I had not thought of before. He treated them kind of like two of the steps in a three-step process. I got the idea he was saying we are to proclaim the gospel as a somewhat general task, then persuade specific unbelievers, and then cultivate believers."[1]

"Your questions are interesting, Di," Greg continued, smiling at his wife, "because Engel believed that we do have some part in the persuading, although the Holy Spirit is the main Person responsible for that task. Let me run and get the book."

As Greg trotted down the hall to retrieve his book, Bern commented, "Yes, the Holy Spirit has to be working in a heart for someone to believe, but Paul also said, 'Therefore, knowing the fear of the Lord, we persuade others' in 2 Corinthians 5:11. We don't want to be pushy or overbearing, but apparently there is a sense in that we do need to persuade."

Bible Reference:
2 Corinthians 5:11

"Look at those kids go!" Greg exclaimed arriving back at the glassed-in observation deck, book in hand. "They love these slides."

"And they love the water," Diana added, laughing as the kids came up out of the water after their train dumped into the warm pool. "This was a great place to come."

Bible Reference:
Matthew 28

"Now, let's see," said Greg, thumbing through Engel's book as he plopped down in the overstuffed chair. "Yeah, here on page 44 Engel is referring to Jesus' command to make disciples of all nations in Matthew 28. Okay. He says,

... we are given the privilege of sharing the Good News and persuading people everywhere to become followers of the Master. People are not merely to be exposed to the message but are to be won, whenever possible, for an eternal cause.

The Great Commission is not fulfilled, however, merely by proclaiming the message and exposing another to its claims. The convert is to be baptized and taught to observe all that Christ has commanded the Church. Thus, becoming a

1 James F. Engel & H. Wilbert Norton, *What's Gone Wrong with the Harvest?* (Grand Rapids: Zondervan, 1975)

disciple is a process continuing over a life span as believers are conformed to the image of Christ (Phil. 1:6). The Church has a definite obligation to cultivate the new believer, helping him or her to grow in the faith.

Bible Reference:
Philippians 1:6

It appears, then, that the Great Commission contains three related but distinctly different communication mandates: (1) to proclaim the message; (2) to persuade the unbeliever; and (3) to cultivate the believer. Part of the problem with the harvest comes from fuzzy thinking at precisely this point because of a tendency to blur the essential distinctions between these communication functions.[2]

Then he says Figure 3, a chart a student of his suggested and then Engel developed over the next few years, is significant. He thinks the reason it is so important is that it helps to "place these communication ministries [proclaiming, persuading, and cultivating] in the perspective of the spiritual decision process that is followed as one becomes a believer in Jesus Christ and grows in the faith.'"[3]

"Let's see that," Bern responded, moving across the room. For the next several minutes, the foursome crowded around Engel's book to get a better look at the chart on page 45.

They nudged each other, pointed at steps unbelievers take on the chart, and commented—all the while gaining a better understanding of the fact that unbelievers move through a process on their journey to faith. As they talked, they realized some other steps could be added to the chart as the unbeliever moved from darkness to light. They also wanted to incorporate the verses they had been studying, so the four *good soil* students pulled their chairs closer to the coffee table and began to draw their own chart. As they did so, they also were learning that gospel communicators must change roles during the process if they want to help move unbelievers along the scale.

... unbelievers move through a process on their journey to faith.

Exercise #3:

On the next page, there is an example of what the first draft of their Good Soil scale looked like. Study it for a few minutes before reading more so you can understand what our foursome is learning.

2 Ibid.
3 Ibid.

Download at:
www.GoodSoil
.com/Scale

Human Spiritual Responses		Our Roles	God's Roles	
Serves in leadership roles	+12			
Spiritual giftedness confirmed	+11			
Disciples new & immature believers	+10			
Deepens Bible/theology knowledge	+9			
Participates in Christian service	+8			
Identifies with Christ in baptism	+7			
Identifies with other believers	+6			
Witnesses to unbelievers	+5			
Experiences sin & confession	+4			
Begins Bible reading & prayer	+3			
Gains assurance of salvation	+2			
Experiences initial life changes	+1	Discipling	Sanctification	
Repents and trusts Jesus			Regeneration	
Counts cost of a faith response	-1			
Confronted with a faith response	-2			
Senses personal spiritual conviction	-3			
Understands some gospel concepts*	-4			
Interested in Jesus and the gospel	-5			
Exposed to other Christian concepts	-6			
Realizes there is only one true God	-7			
Vulnerable to false religious beliefs	-8			
Seeks to fill personal spiritual void	-9			
Senses personal spiritual emptiness	-10			
Aware of higher Power or powers	-11		Conviction	
Born with a God-Vacuum	-12	Evangelizing	General and Special Revelation	

Luke 8:15 — Mark 4:20 — Matthew 13:23

Ninety minutes passed before the busy bunch pushed back to admire
their work. There was much to absorb as they looked at this Good Soil Scale.
They realized there might be more to add as they continued to study.

"So we're saying that everyone in the world is somewhere on this
continuum?" Diana asked more than stated.

"That's right, and where they fall on the scale will affect where they are in their understanding of the gospel and even how they would respond to a gospel witness," Greg answered. "For example, Mr. Negative Eleven is aware of a Supreme Being or Higher Power, but he has no clear awareness of the gospel of Jesus Christ."

> *Where people fall on the scale will affect where they are in their understanding of the gospel and even how they would respond to a gospel witness.*

"And uh," interjected Bern, searching for something while moving his finger up the chart, "Miss Minus Four is beginning to have some awareness of the gospel but not necessarily grasping its implications." He paused as if something just occurred to him. "Humph. Only at negative three and up are individuals ready for a challenge to trust Christ as Savior. A realization of that fact would keep us from encouraging a decision right away from some people."

"What do you mean?" Miriam asked.

"Well, last week when I was talking with that gentleman at *Rathaus*, I realized that he wasn't even sure that God existed. But since I had shared the gospel, and I was always taught that we should push for a decision, I did. I'm afraid I turned him off more than anything."

Rathaus:
city hall

Just then a drenched, shivering Misha, the youngest Sämann, approached the group hugging himself to keep warm. *"Entschuldigung sie bitte, Mama."*

"*Ja, Liebchen?*" Miriam asked as she rubbed his upper arms.

"*Was fûr sandwiches haben sie?*" Misha responded.

Entschuldigung sie bitte, Mama:
Excuse me, Mommy

"What kind of sandwiches do I have? Are you hungry, little buddy?"

Misha nodded affirmatively, and everyone laughed.

"Me, too," agreed Greg. What do you say we break for lunch?"

Everyone agreed that it was time, so the development of the scale would have to wait until after noon.

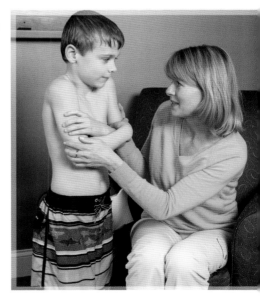

Diana needed time to think. So as they split up, she was glad Miri was responsible for today's noon meal, and Greg was going to collect their kids and get them dressed for lunch. The time together had been stimulating, and the scale was turning out to be an interesting tool for understanding how people may indeed move from not knowing anything about God on up to trusting

Christ as Savior, but something was bothering her. Could she put it into words?

She leaned against the railing high above the water slides and watched through the thick glass pane as Greg shuttled their two older ones into the shower rooms. *Good soil*, she thought. *Yes, Jesus described some as good soil—the ones who accepted the Word. But there were other soils as well. Thorny, rocky, the pathway where the birds picked up the seed and ate it. What about the people represented by those soils? They don't believe, but why? There will always be people who don't believe. Is there anything we can do about that? Why did Jesus tell this parable anyway? What was His purpose? Was it simply to let us know that not all will believe? Is there another lesson here for us?*

Thoughts were coming a mile a minute. She was confused but confident that Jesus had another lesson in mind that she was missing. Sure, many Bible scholars down through the ages had learned and taught many lessons from this passage, but it seemed there was something there, something just out of reach. Something that a little meditation would turn up.

Diana smacked her hands on the railing, then threw them in the air, a big smile on her face. No words came out of her mouth, but some of the swimmers down below could not miss the spectacle and cocked their heads sideways as they looked at her curiously. They looked around in the pool, thinking that someone she knew must have just won a race or waved to her or something. When they looked back at the observation deck, she was gone. She was headed to lunch with her eyes a little brighter, her step a little lighter in her eagerness to share an insight with the team.

What Can We Do about It?
Because Seeds Fall All over the Place

"Preparation of the soil!" blurted out Diana, a grin on her face, as the team began their afternoon session.

"Excuse me?" a surprised Greg asked his wife, then chuckled, wondering at her enthusiasm.

"Yes, tell us what you're so excited about," Miriam gushed, the dance in her eyes only matched by Diana's. She was such an empathetic person that she easily got caught up in another's excitement.

"Well," Diana started slowly, wanting to express her jumbled thoughts clearly. "I really liked what Engel said about proclaiming, persuading, and cultivating. I'm beginning to understand that we, the human communicators, are to *proclaim* the gospel while the Holy Spirit convicts. Then we are to *persuade* once 'sufficient biblical awareness and … recognition (of the sin problem) have been achieved …'[4] Then, of course, when a new believer trusts Christ as Savior he must be followed up, or cultivated. I mean, after all, he is a new creature; his life has just begun; he must be cared for so that the new life is not snuffed out. These are three key activities in which we must be involved, according to Engel. But I was wondering if there isn't another piece of the process that we haven't mentioned, something before the proclaiming."

"What could come before proclaiming?" a puzzled Miriam ventured.

"I don't know, maybe it is part of the proclaiming, but what I'm thinking is that the soil has to be prepared. I don't know any passages where Jesus commands us to prepare the soil—maybe there are some. But couldn't that be at least one of the lessons we should get from this parable? Think about it. There is wayside soil, rocky soil, thorny, and … ?

"Good soil," the remaining three said in unison.

"Right, and how did the soil get that way?" Diana replied, sure that she should be getting through, but silence and blank faces were the only answers she got to her question.

"Somebody tilled it!" she blurted. "It's almost so obvious that we don't see it, but before the sowing of the seed began, the farmer was already there ahead of

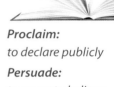

Proclaim:
to declare publicly

Persuade:
to cause to believe

Cultivate:
to foster growth

Prepare:
to make ready

The soil has to be prepared.

4 Ibid, 46.

time *preparing* the soil. That's the only reason there was any *good soil* in the first place. The pathway wasn't prepared; the soil outside the field where there are rocks and thorns wasn't prepared …" Now she slowed down and said each word deliberately. "… But the field was."

After letting that sink in a bit, Diana continued. "So here is my question: Shouldn't we include in our evangelism some kind of *preparing* ministry—whatever we want to call it—so the proclaiming and persuading can be more fruitful? In other words, shouldn't we prepare the soil so we can have *good soil* faith responses?"

> ## Shouldn't we include in our evangelism some kind of preparing ministry—whatever we call it—so the proclaiming and persuading can be more fruitful?

Again, silence. But this time it was not a confused silence. There were grins on every face as they looked around at each other. Heads were spinning. It was simple yet so profound. Certainly they had done some preparing of soil in the past, but including it like this in a strategy—brilliant!

"I'm sure someone has thought of this before," Greg started, "but as an application from this passage—emphasizing the need to prepare the soil— I've never heard it." Turning to his wife, he said proudly, "Great job, Honey."

"It's an obvious assumption to the farmer. He's got to get out there and till the soil before he tries to sow," commented Bern.

Human Spiritual Responses		Our Roles
Gains assurance of salvation	+2	
Experiences initial life changes	+1	Discipling
Repents and trusts Jesus		
Counts cost of a faith response	-1	
Confronted with a faith response	-2	
Senses personal spiritual conviction	-3	
Understands some gospel concepts*	-4	
Interested in Jesus and the gospel	-5	
Exposed to other Christian concepts	-6	
Realizes there is only one true God	-7	
Vulnerable to false religious beliefs	-8	
Seeks to fill personal spiritual void	-9	
Senses personal spiritual emptiness	-10	
Aware of higher Power or powers	-11	
Born with a God-Vacuum	-12	Evangelizing

Greg came back with, "Maybe we are so far removed from biblical culture that we just don't realize the inherent implications."

"Or maybe it was obvious to Jesus' first-century hearers," interjected Miriam.

Almost simultaneously, the group turned to their Good Soil Scale. They could see this concept had to be incorporated somehow. On the bottom half of the chart as one of *Our Roles* they had *Evangelizing*. On the top half, *Discipling*. The question was where to put *preparing* or *preparing the soil*, or some such thing. Where would it fit into the unbeliever's journey toward trusting Christ? Or maybe the better

38

question, since preparing obviously came first, where should the *evangelizing* stage go?

Bern spoke first. "I'm just thinking out loud here. Jump in whenever. Born with a God-Vacuum is where we all start. In other words, God has created everyone with an inherent need, even a desire, for Him. Then, although we can have a part in moving someone to being aware of *the* Higher Power—the one true living God—through proclamation, it is really God's role to show Himself through general revelation. There's nothing we can do about that."

Greg jumped in. "Yes, the proclaimed Word helps people see who God is, but God has made Himself known through creation. Psalm 19:1 says, 'The heavens declare the glory of God.'"

Bible Reference:
Psalm 19:1

"Right," Bern agreed. "And even though people can sense a spiritual empti-ness without believers around, the Spirit in us—changing us and making Christ attractive through godly lives—can help create a sense of a need for God."

Miriam was following well. "So that takes us up to at least," she said slowly, scanning the scale, "negative 9."

"But it looks like negative 7 is where proclamation starts, when unbe-lievers are 'exposed to biblical monotheism,'" pondered Diana.

Greg became quiet. His expression showed that he was deep in thought, his eyes darting up and down the first half of the chart. All eyes turned to him when it became obvious that Diana was searching his face for affirmation.

"I think you're right, Sweetie, but hear me carefully for a second, because

Monotheism:
the belief that
there is only one
God

I'm not *at all* saying you're wrong," Greg said with his eyes still on the chart. "I really like this concept of preparing the soil. You made a phenomenal catch. But, …" Greg paused for effect, "… what if we continue to have *evangelizing* as our one major task all through the bottom half of the chart, but divide it into subtasks something like this?"

Greg quickly sketched a bracket from -8 down past -12; another bracket from above -5 to below -7, and a third from above -1 to below -4. Then, at the point of the lowest bracket he wrote Tilling Evan-gelism; at the point of the middle bracket, Planting Evangelism; and at the top bracket, Reaping Evange-lism.

Human Spiritual Responses	
Counts cost of a faith response	-1
Reaping Evangelism	-2
Se…	-3
Understands some gospel concepts*	-4
Interested in Jesus and the gospel	-5
Ex… **Planting Evangelism**	-6
Realizes there is only one true God	-7
Vulnerable to false religious beliefs	-8
Seeks to fill personal spiritual void	-9
Se… **Tilling Evangelism**	-10
Aware of higher Power or powers	-11
Born with a God-Vacuum	-12

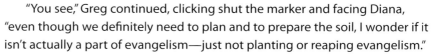

Tilling Evangelism: *modeling of the Christian life, loving unbelievers as Christ loves them, praying for God to move them*

"You see," Greg continued, clicking shut the marker and facing Diana, "even though we definitely need to plan and to prepare the soil, I wonder if it isn't actually a part of evangelism—just not planting or reaping evangelism."

Miriam joined in. "Yes, I think I get what you're saying. Tilling Evangelism would be our modeling of the Christian life, loving unbelievers as Christ loves them ..."

"And praying for God to move them," interjected Diana.

"Yes, and we even can have conversations with people about their worldview at this stage, too," Bern added. But before he was done, Greg was finishing his thought. "All the while praying and hoping to see our friends move up the scale."

"Now, just to make it a little clearer," Miriam said, rising and crossing to the flip chart while taking the cap off a different color marker, "while participating in Tilling Evangelism what was it we said we should be doing? One thing was to pray, right?"

"Yes, and modeling, and loving," Diana added.

Bern finished the list adding, "And challenging our unbelieving friends' worldviews."

Miriam wrote those tasks under Tilling Evangelism and then asked, "If those are tasks under the role of tilling evangelism, what are the tasks under the role of planting evangelism?"

"Well," started Greg, "at -7 people at least are exposed to monotheism. I think here is where we have to begin teaching some gospel concepts. Once people accept the fact that there is one God, and we hope they are beginning to see that He is the God of the Bible, we have to help them get the foundational truths of the gospel."

Planting Evangelism: *teaching some gospel concepts, establish the uniqueness of Jesus*

While the group waited for another idea, Bern developed a quizzical look. He was thinking hard about what Greg had just said. He was just about to say something when Diana spoke up with an idea. "I think, too, that we need to establish the uniqueness of Jesus here. Our unbelieving friends have to be confronted with the fact that there is 'no other name under heaven ... by which we must be saved' according to Acts 4:12."

Bible Reference: *Acts 4:12*

"That's good. Very good," Bern responded. "Let's get both of those down on paper. But before moving on I'd like to go back to what Greg said: the foundational truths of the gospel. What do you suppose those are? Now hold on before you think that I am *nicht informiert* (ignorant). I know, we all know what the gospel is. But we said yesterday that it is important for unbelievers to really *understand* the gospel, right? Well, if we were to take from all of Scripture some basic gospel concepts we believe a person needs to know and understand to be able to make a *good soil* response, what would they be?"

As Bern let that sink in a little, an idea came to mind. He said, "Let's all put down on paper what we think are the basic gospel concepts a person must understand in order to trust Christ as Savior. We'll work individually and then compare our answers."

"How many should we come up with?" asked Miriam. "Three? Four? Forty-seven?"

"Let's not think about how many just now. Let's just think through what someone needs to understand regardless of the number of concepts."

"Okay."

"Good."

"Let's do it."

The group went to work. It was difficult because their minds naturally went to familiar outlines they had learned in evangelism training classes and used in well-known tracts. But they tried to clear their minds of preconceived ideas. They attempted to think, in simple terms, what a person needs to understand to truly

Exercise #4:

What do you think are basic gospel concepts a person needs to understand in order to trust Jesus as Savior? Remember, "suniemi" means to comprehend, mentally grasp, or see how it all fits together. Therefore, you are trying to come up with everything a person must know to make a good soil faith response.

trust Christ as Savior. After a short time they each read their lists, compared, discussed, and agreed on eight essential gospel concepts.

"How do we feel about that?" asked Bern. "Are those our eight basic gospel concepts? How about if someone walks us through them?"

"I'll do it. Miri, you help me if I get stuck," Diana said tentatively.

"All right. Go for it, Di," Miriam answered.

"Okay," Diana started slowly, methodically, studying the words on the flip chart as she spoke. "The all-powerful Creator **God** of the Bible created **man** in His own image and made him a responsible being." She emphasized each concept and pointed to the representative words on the flip chart as she said them. "Man was to name the animals, work the garden, and eat of every tree except the forbidden one. But man chose his own way, disobeying the command. God calls that **sin**. As God warned, sin brought His judgment— **death**, or separation. Adam and Eve experienced spiritual death immediately and physical death some time later. Since we are descendants of Adam and Eve, we too are spiritually dead and will suffer physical death; 'it is appointed for man to die once.' (Hebrews 9:27) Eternal death—separation from God forever—also awaits us as part of God's judgment upon sin."

❶ God
❷ Man
❸ Sin
❹ Death

Miriam decided to give Diana a break and interrupted with "But." Turning to Diana with a nod and a smile, she said, "You may be seated, ma'am." Addressing the others she continued, "But, because God loves us so much He gave His Son, **Jesus**, to die in our place. He paid the price of our sin when He sacrificed Himself on the **cross** and made it possible to have a right relationship with God again. All who place their **faith** in Jesus and what He did on the cross can have **life** everlasting; they will live with God forever, worshipping Him in His glory."

Bible Reference:
Hebrews 9:27

❺ Christ
❻ Cross
❼ Faith
❽ Life

Greg and Bern erupted into mock applause, alternating between clapping and making "thunderous" applause sounds with their hands cupped to their mouths.

Available from:
www.GoodSoil.com

Bern exclaimed, "Very good. Not only did you ladies do a fine job of summarizing the gospel concepts, but I think we have gotten the essence.

"And I like them in that order. When one shares those basic concepts in that order, he or she is giving a chronological presentation of God's redemptive story. We can add more verses or take some out. We can have more Bible story illustrations or fewer, but we will have

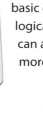

42

shared what we learned about God and His plan as it has been revealed in the Bible and over time."

"Yes," said Greg slowly. He seemed to be chewing on something. "You know," he continued, "that's how God gave us revelation—in story form and bit by bit, slowly revealing more and more over time. We may not be able to deal with this right now, but we should do some thinking about that later."

God gave us His revelation in story form, bit by bit, slowly revealing more and more over time.

"What do you mean?" Diana queried.

"Well, this chronological idea, telling the gospel as a story, making sure all the pieces are there. God gave it to us in story form, but we want to put it all in boxes, systematize it. In this postmodern world we live in, stories would be more effective. Maybe we can come back to this idea later. I'm just saying that what Bern said about the concepts being *chronological* in order hit home with me."

Chronological: *arranged in the order that things happened*

"Good, I think you're right," said Bern. "Let's try to finish up with the bottom half of this scale before we break to spend time with the kids on the slides. I still haven't gone on the big one that finishes up out of doors."

"You haven't?" Diana asked. "It's fun. As you start down, it's all black with little pinholes of light above like stars. It spins a lot, taking your breath away, but as it straightens out and drops you into the pool. The cool outside air clears your head when you swim under the divider back inside the dome. It's my favorite. You'll want to keep most of your body underwater to keep warm as you swim."

"It sounds great. My kids can't stop talking about it. But, before we can go *down* the slides we have to move *up* our scale a bit more. So," Bern recapped, "in level one, or Tilling Evangelism, we model, love, pray, and begin to challenge core worldviews. Correct?"

"Yes," Miriam jumped in, "and in Planting Evangelism we teach gospel concepts. Altogether now, say: God, man, sin, death, Christ, cross, faith, life." By the time she reached "sin" everyone was reciting with her.

"Right," said Bern, eager to deal with level three. "So what are our roles in this third level of evangelism? What should we be doing when our unbelieving friends are moving from negative four to negative one?"

1. Considers cost of a faith response.

2. Confronted with a faith response.

3. Senses personal spiritual conviction.

4. Understands some gospel concepts.

"Hmm," the friends echoed in unison. They looked at the chart. There they saw phrases they had listed beside the numbers an hour before.

All at once, each one had a response:

"We ought to try to clarify the gospel and deal with issues people have."

"Maybe we should help them see the gospel is real and relevant to them."

"If there's ever a time for us to persuade, it's now. Now that they have the essential gospel knowledge, we can challenge them to take a step of faith."

"Hold on! One at a time!" replied Bern, holding his hands up as if trying to slow down a group trying to get through a turnstile all at once. "Ladies first. Miri?"

"What's the matter? 'Have you only two ears'?" Miriam chuckled, quoting Bern's favorite phrase to use when their children would come in excited from school, each talking a mile a minute. "As I looked at the steps an unbeliever is moving through at these stages, I thought it would be good to listen to them and be ready to clarify anything they don't understand."

Shooting a knowing smile her way, Bern said, "Excellent!" and wrote *Clarify* under *Reaping Evangelism*. "Di, how about you? What did you come up with?"

"In short, I said to bring it home. In other words, make sure they know the gospel is for them right where they live," Diana restated.

"Good. Can we call that *Personalize*?" Bern asked.

"Yeah, that's the idea," Diana responded.

"Okay, buddy, it's your turn, "Bern said, turning to Greg. "What have you got for us, *freundchen*?"

Reaping Evangelism:

clarify, personalize, persuade,

make sure they understand before we look for a faith response

"Well," replied Greg, "I think now is the time to persuade. They've come up the scale and they understand the gospel. Let's do what we can at this point to 'persuade men' as Paul said."

Bernard finished writing *Persuade* on the scale as Diana commented, "These three tasks are really related. We want to make sure they understand before we look for a faith response. If I understand Engel, I think this is one of his emphases. But as we do that, we help them see how the gospel really relates to them and *then* urge them to respond."

"It's kind of like the pieces of a lesson plan: know, feel, and do," added Miriam. "When we're teaching, we desire a trio of results from our students. We want them to really *know* something new from the Bible. We want them to *feel* happy, or sad, or responsible, or whatever the text requires. That's personalizing it. And we want them to *do* something: respond in obedience with whatever action is appropriate. When I look at evangelism this way, it's clearer to me what I need to do and how I need to do it."

> *We want them to really know something new from the Bible. … And we want them to do something: respond in obedience with whatever action is appropriate.*

"It is certainly helping me, too," Bern agreed. "So here is our E&D Scale, or I should say our Good Soil Evangelism and Discipleship Scale. This should help us understand not only the process that an unbeliever goes through in trusting Christ but also our changing roles and our partnership with God along the way."

There were nods, words of affirmation, as the men slapped each other's back. A feeling of excitement was in the air. But Diana fell silent sooner than the rest, and as the congratulating died down, it was obvious that something was bothering her.

"What's wrong?" asked Greg.

"Well, this scale is great," Diana started in. "But doesn't it show us what happens—this moving up the scale—with people that are *good* soil? After all, that's what we named it: Good Soil. But won't we always have people representing the other types of soils?"

"Yes, we will," Bernard responded. "Jesus makes clear in his parable that there are at least four types of responses, or variations of them, from people."

"Well, what about *those* people. Will they never believe? Do we have to throw the seed around and lose, what, 75 percent of it on people who will never believe?" Diana asked, clearly frustrated, holding back the tears.

The Good Soil E&D Scale

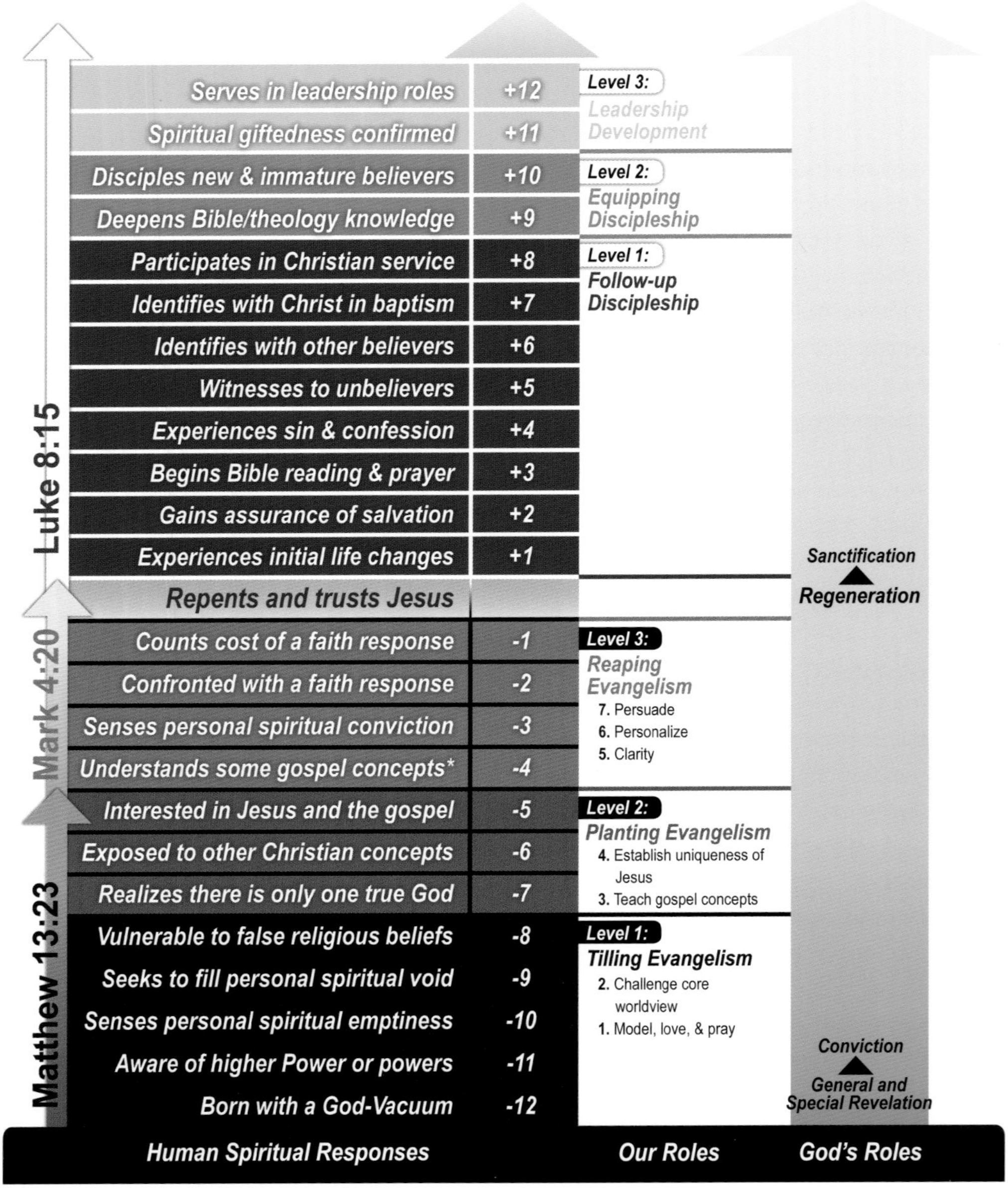

Human Spiritual Responses		Our Roles	God's Roles
Serves in leadership roles	+12	**Level 3:** Leadership Development	
Spiritual giftedness confirmed	+11		
Disciples new & immature believers	+10	**Level 2:** Equipping Discipleship	
Deepens Bible/theology knowledge	+9		
Participates in Christian service	+8	**Level 1:** Follow-up Discipleship	
Identifies with Christ in baptism	+7		
Identifies with other believers	+6		
Witnesses to unbelievers	+5		
Experiences sin & confession	+4		
Begins Bible reading & prayer	+3		
Gains assurance of salvation	+2		
Experiences initial life changes	+1		Sanctification ▲ Regeneration
Repents and trusts Jesus			
Counts cost of a faith response	-1	**Level 3:** Reaping Evangelism 7. Persuade 6. Personalize 5. Clarity	
Confronted with a faith response	-2		
Senses personal spiritual conviction	-3		
Understands some gospel concepts*	-4		
Interested in Jesus and the gospel	-5	**Level 2:** Planting Evangelism 4. Establish uniqueness of Jesus 3. Teach gospel concepts	
Exposed to other Christian concepts	-6		
Realizes there is only one true God	-7		
Vulnerable to false religious beliefs	-8	**Level 1:** Tilling Evangelism 2. Challenge core worldview 1. Model, love, & pray	
Seeks to fill personal spiritual void	-9		
Senses personal spiritual emptiness	-10		
Aware of higher Power or powers	-11		Conviction ▲
Born with a God-Vacuum	-12		General and Special Revelation

Left margin labels: Luke 8:15 · Mark 4:20 · Matthew 13:23

Basic gospel concepts = God, man, sin, death, Christ, cross, faith, and life.

The original concept for this scale was created by Viggo Sogaard and later revised by James F. Engel and called the Engel Scale.

The four fell silent. Is that the way it had to be? Was this in essence a sad parable? Could they count on the fact that most of their efforts would be in vain? What about God's promise in Isaiah that His Word would not return empty?

Then Greg started, slowly at first, but gaining strength and confidence as he spoke, convinced that what he was saying was true. "The seed in the parable is the Word, and God has promised in Isaiah 55:10 and 11 that 'as the rain and the snow come down from heaven and do not return there but water the earth, making it bring forth and sprout, giving seed to the sower and bread to the eater, so shall my word be that goes out from my mouth; it shall not return to me empty, but it shall accomplish that which I purpose.' The snow and rain have multiple purposes; they make the earth bud and flourish. And the earth flourishes with more than one purpose: seed for the sower and bread for the eater. In the same way God has more than one purpose for His Word. We may not always see immediate fruit. But what about the snow on the mountains? Does it have immediate action? No, it takes a long time for it to melt and run down the mountain, watering the ground.

Bible Reference:
Isaiah 55:10-11

"When God's Word is proclaimed, it is doing what He wants it to do. This takes time. Sometimes, as Paul said to the Corinthians in 1 Corinthians 3:6, one plants, another waters, and another reaps. Jesus told the disciples in John 4 that they were reaping where others had toiled. I believe one of the reasons Jesus shared the parable of the soils was so we would work at getting people to the point of being *good soil*. It is not a fatalistic parable, emphasizing that only some (25 percent) will respond. It is a parable that teaches us to prepare the soil so more and more will at least make *good soil* decisions, and possibly, more and more will respond positively. Sadly, some will still reject Jesus and His offer of eternal life, but if we share the essential gospel elements, at least they will be responding with a better understanding of God and His story.

Bible References:
1 Corinthians 3:6
John 4

> ***When God's Word is proclaimed, it is doing what He wants it to do.***

"Someone may start out as rocky or thorny soil, but just as you pointed out, Diana, we need to prepare that soil: work with it, separate out the rocks, pull the weeds, till it, until one day it is *good soil* and the seed that is planted can take root and grow.

47

Liebe macht erfinderisch:
Love will find a way.

"The Germans say, *Liebe macht erfinderisch*. As we prayerfully participate in Tilling Evangelism by loving people, and Planting Evangelism through sharing the Word with them, I believe we can trust God to allow us to participate in Reaping Evangelism—see people make *good soil* faith responses. And I am convinced that what we are learning from this parable will enable us to see more fruit than we have before. The Holy Spirit can use our lives and Christ's love in us to change bad soil into *good soil*."

"Amen,. "I think you're right." "May God make it so," the others responded.

"How about we pray again now, then go spend some time with the kids?" asked Bernard. "Maybe we can each look over the scale again and meditate on it a bit before we go to bed."

The group had a good time of prayer thanking God for insights and asking Him to continue to teach them over the next couple of days. Even though Greg had just given a rousing speech as they finished up, it was he who, while walking silently hand in hand with Diana back to their room, was thinking. *We sure have discovered some truths we were not aware of before, but does it make a difference? Will a better understanding of the parable of the soils and this Good Soil Evangelism and Discipleship Scale be enough to radically change our ministry? Will it be enough to produce long-lasting fruit on a larger scale than we have yet experienced? Will it be enough to keep us here, in Germany?*

He hoped and prayed it would be so.[5]

5 You may be having some of these same questions. Visit www.GoodSoil.com to discover more about Good Soil principles or send your questions to Info@GoodSoil.com.

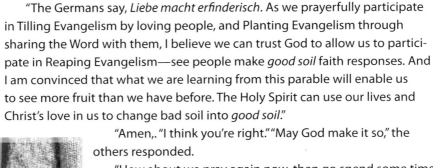

Exercise #5:

We began this chapter asking "Where do the seeds fall?" Greg & Diana and Bern & Miri have learned that the seeds will always fall on all four soils, but that with prayer and work people may move from one soil type to another. They've learned that tilling evangelism can move people up the scale so that planting evangelism can be more effective, which should lead to reaping evangelism. **Study the scale so that you are familiar with it before moving to chapter 4 to discover what the group will learn next.**

The Good Soil E&D Scale

Luke 8:15	Human Spiritual Responses		Our Roles	God's Roles
	Serves in leadership roles	+12	**Level 3:** Leadership Development	
	Spiritual giftedness confirmed	+11		
	Disciples new & immature believers	+10	**Level 2:** Equipping Discipleship	
	Deepens Bible/theology knowledge	+9		
	Participates in Christian service	+8	**Level 1:** Follow-up Discipleship	
	Identifies with Christ in baptism	+7		
	Identifies with other believers	+6		
	Witnesses to unbelievers	+5		
	Experiences sin & confession	+4		
	Begins Bible reading & prayer	+3		
	Gains assurance of salvation	+2		
	Experiences initial life changes	+1		▲ Sanctification
	Repents and trusts Jesus			▲ Regeneration
Mark 4:20	Counts cost of a faith response	-1	**Level 3:** Reaping Evangelism 7. Persuade 6. Personalize 5. Clarity	
	Confronted with a faith response	-2		
	Senses personal spiritual conviction	-3		
	Understands some gospel concepts*	-4		
	Interested in Jesus and the gospel	-5	**Level 2:** Planting Evangelism 4. Establish uniqueness of Jesus 3. Teach gospel concepts	
	Exposed to other Christian concepts	-6		
	Realizes there is only one true God	-7		
Matthew 13:23	Vulnerable to false religious beliefs	-8	**Level 1:** Tilling Evangelism 2. Challenge core worldview 1. Model, love, & pray	
	Seeks to fill personal spiritual void	-9		
	Senses personal spiritual emptiness	-10		
	Aware of higher Power or powers	-11		▲ Conviction
	Born with a God-Vacuum	-12		▲ General and Special Revelation

Basic gospel concepts = God, man, sin, death, Christ, cross, faith, and life.

The original concept for this scale was created by Viggo Sogaard and later revised by James F. Engel and called the Engel Scale.

How Should We Sow? (Part 1)
Initial Contact and Relational Evangelism

Greg rolled over and looked at the empty space in the bed. The smell of toast and coffee told him where Diana was. He was surprised he had slept so soundly and had not heard her get up. Apparently the questions about the long-term value of their study so far were not enough to keep him awake. It had been another good night's sleep for him—two in a row now. Whether it was the comfortable bed at the aparthotel, or sliding in the warm water with the family, or the fact that he was relaxing and not experiencing the nervousness about their missionary career, Greg wasn't sure. But he could get used to this.

As Greg stepped into the kitchen with sleep in his eyes and his short hair sticking out awkwardly, Diana kidded good-naturedly, "Aw, there's the handsome man I married!"

Without a word and a silly grin on his face, Greg quickly wet his hair down, grabbed her waist, dipped her low, and planted a kiss on her mouth.

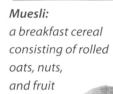

Muesli: a breakfast cereal consisting of rolled oats, nuts, and fruit

The two older kids, eating muesli, shrieked, "Aw, *Papa*!" Julie covered her eyes with her hands, while Kaylie continued her complaint. "Do you have to do that in front of us? And so early in the morning?" In the high chair Allie giggled, kicked her legs up and down, and popped another Oaty-O into her mouth.

The fact of the matter was the girls liked to see their father show his love for their mother. They felt secure in their home even though they were an ocean away from their parents' homeland. Their parents loved each other, supplied their needs, and taught them about their heavenly Father who cared for them wherever they were on this earth.

"Oh, all right!" Greg laughed. "Life is so difficult for you, isn't it? How about if I just tickle you instead?" he threatened.

Letting out shrill screams, the girls began to run, and Greg was after them.

"*Nein, nein!*" they shouted as they dodged this way and that around the apartment. It was natural for them to answer in either German or English. They were happy in Germany even though they sensed at times *Mama und Papa* were struggling a bit. After a few minutes Greg managed to corral the two older girls, laughing hysterically from his tickling. Knowing too much of a good thing can be a problem, he let them catch their breath.

Little Allie had been twisting and turning in her high chair, not wanting to miss a moment of the chase. When it was over, she plopped her diapered bottom back down on the seat, speared the last two Oaty-Os with a finger from each hand and popped them into her mouth. As Allie munched on them contentedly, Julie whined, "Do we have to leave tomorrow? It's so much fun here."

Diana took Allie out of the high chair and joined them in the living room. "Yes, we have to go back to Frankfurt tomorrow, but we have another whole day here at Monte Mare. What do you want to do today?"

The next few minutes were filled with a detailed itinerary: "four times on this slide" and "five times on that slide." They wanted to get under all the different waterfalls and see which was more soothing on their backs—and which ones hurt the most. Some of the "falls" shot the water out with such force that it stung their skin. The girls would run races in the big pool with the Sämann boys, and, of course, they wanted to play one more game of Monopoly®.

"Sounds like a good last day," Greg encouraged. "Let's have our devotions before I get a quick shower. *"Onkel Bern und Tante Miri* will be waiting for us."

"Onk Ben, Tant Mi," tried Allie, bouncing up and down with glee on her mother's knee.

"Yes, let's start," urged Kaylie. "I told Gustav that we would meet him and Misha at nine o'clock."

"That's fine," affirmed Greg. "We should have plenty of time. I'm reading this morning from Acts 16:25 to 34."

> *About midnight Paul and Silas were praying and singing hymns to God, and the prisoners were listening to them, and suddenly there was a great earthquake, so that the foundations of the prison were shaken. And immediately all the doors were opened, and everyone's bonds were unfastened. When the jailer woke and saw that the prison doors were open, he drew his sword and was about to kill himself, supposing that the prisoners had escaped. But Paul cried with a loud voice, "Do not harm yourself, for we are all here."*

Bible Reference:
Acts 16:25-34

Greg acted out the text as he usually did when reading to the kids. He used inflection and a different voice for each person and with his free hand drew a sword or whatever was appropriate for the verses. The narrative continued.

> *And the jailer called for lights and rushed in, and trembling with fear he fell down before Paul and Silas. Then he brought them out and said, "Sirs, what must I do to be saved?"*

Greg was on his knees now. Then he jumped up as he quoted Paul's response,

> *"Believe in the Lord Jesus, and you will be saved, you and your household." And they spoke the word of the Lord to him and to all who were in his house. And he took them the same hour of the night and washed their wounds; and he was baptized at once, he and all his family. Then he brought them up into*

his house and set food before them. And he rejoiced along with his entire household that he had believed in God.

"Papa," Kaylie asked thoughtfully, "if we had an earthquake here, would people believe when we tell them about Jesus? I mean, the jailer believed the first time he was told about Jesus. He even asked what he needed to do to be saved. It seems like you and Mama and *Onkel Bern und Tante Miri* tell people about Jesus, and they don't even care. Would an earthquake help?"

Liebling:
Love, darling,
honey

"Well, *Liebling*, it just might—although I don't know if we want to wish for one. But, you know, this man was in a crisis that made him think about what was important in life. The earthquake freed the prisoners from their chains so he thought they had all escaped. He was responsible for them, and Roman law said the jailer would be tortured and killed if his prisoners got away. That's why he drew his sword and was ready to kill himself. When Paul stopped him, he was ready to hear what Paul had to say."

Diana added, "People who have a tragedy or a big change in their lives often are more open to the good news about Jesus. So even though we would never wish for an earthquake or a difficult or sad experience, we do want to love people and be ready to help them during those times."

> **People who have a tragedy or a big change in their lives are more open to the good news about Jesus.**

Greg had been looking back at the previous verses in chapter 16, reviewing the rest of the story. He was trying to confirm something that Kaylie's questions brought to his mind. But looking at his watch, and realizing the girls needed to get ready to go meet their friends, he asked, "Who's ready to hit the slides?"

He was bombarded with "Me!" and three hands in the air.

"Okay, then. Let's pray before we get your suits and flip-flops on, and you can go to meet Gustav and Misha. Dear God," he started praying, "thank You for Your Word that teaches us and encourages us. We praise you for saving the Philippian jailer and ask that you would help us to be faithful in sharing the good news with people." After a moment's pause he added, "And that You would save people around us. Draw our friends to Yourself as we tell them about Jesus. In His name we pray, Amen."

Kaylie and Julie repeated the "amen" and even little Allie made an attempt. The next few

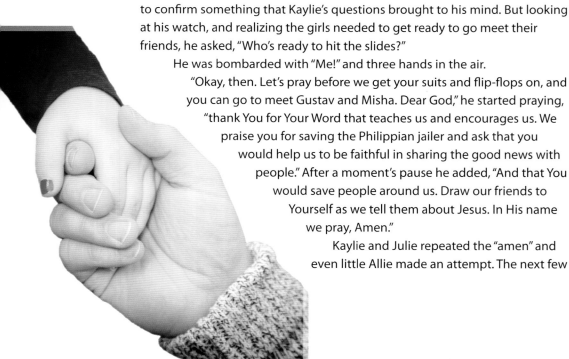

minutes were filled with finding swimsuits and flip-flops—including that elusive one that required searching high and low. Finally they were ready to head to the "big pool," the agreed-upon meeting point.

Greg helped with the kids, but while Diana and Amber took them to the pool and he took a quick shower, he was thinking about the Bible verses they had read. As he got dressed his mind went to other passages, wondering if they would shed light on this aspect of evangelism. By the time he got to the adults' meeting place, he was eager to share what he had been thinking.

Guten Morgen:
Good morning

"*Guten Morgen!*" Greg greeted Bern and Miri cheerfully.

"*Morgen.*" "*Guten Morgen*," they replied.

"How did you sleep?" Greg asked. "I had another great night."

"Well, thanks," Bern answered. "The beds here are comfortable. We've been getting some needed rest."

"This has been such a wonderful few days of refueling," added Miriam. "It's been restful, the times with the kids are fun, and our study times have been so beneficial also."

"It has been good," Greg agreed. "Let's spend some time in prayer thanking God and asking Him to continue to direct our time together."

After prayer Greg said, "You'll never believe what Kaylie said in our devotional time this morning. We had read the story of the Philippian jailer, and she piped up, 'If we had an earthquake here, would people believe when we tell them about Jesus?' She was surprised that the jailer believed after hearing the gospel only once. She was hoping that we could somehow see that kind of response in our ministry."

> "If we had an earthquake here, would people believe when we tell them about Jesus?"

"Wow!" Miriam commented. "It looks as if we're not the only ones frustrated with our evangelistic efforts. What did you say to her?"

"Well, I talked about how the crisis he was going through helped prepare him …"

"Prepare the soil?" interrupted Bern.

"Mm-hmm. Good one. And Diana tried to explain how tragedies many times will do that—prepare people or create more interest in spiritual things."

"Fantastic!" exclaimed Miriam. "What a teachable moment that was! Praise God!"

"Yes, it was great. Only He can put moments together like that," said Greg. "But I got to thinking and looking at the passage. Kaylie noticed that the jailer heard once and believed and in her innocence wondered why it couldn't be like that for us. But it wasn't always like that for Paul either. In fact, in the same passage other people may have heard several times before believing.

Bible Reference:
Acts 16:13-18

"Look at this chapter." Greg waited a moment as the rest opened their Bibles to Acts 16, then continued. "Even though we see the jailer responding after hearing only once, in Philippi—the same town, culture, and time—some people needed to hear more often before they believed. Paul began in this city by going to the river where he expected to find people praying (verse 13). He met Lydia and some others.

"Lydia was a God fearer; she had already come to the point of believing in the God of Bible, possibly because Jews from her hometown (Thyatira) had influenced her to believe. Later, while living in a Philippi, the Lord opened Lydia's heart to respond to Paul's message (verse 14).

Diana interjected, "I see. Lydia began to believe, possibly years before, when she turned to the God of the Bible; she began the conversion process. But she was regenerated by the Spirit at a later time (at the river), in another town."

"That's right," commended Greg. She clearly took longer than the jailer to come to Christ. Paul also continued to develop relationships in Philippi after Lydia believed. Verse 16 says, 'As we were going to the place of prayer …' They

had been there at least once, when Lydia believed, but they continued to go back to meet with others. Verse 18 indicates they continued meeting with people in this town 'for many days.'

"Anyway, I got to wondering if there were other passages that might show us an extended proclamation ministry. I'd like to see if we can find some. You see, we've been talking about *what* we need to share with people—the eight essential gospel elements—and we have learned so much. But I'm wondering if we can learn a little more about *how* we ought to share. What kinds of approaches should we take?"

"But didn't we discuss *how* we need to share the gospel when we said we need to consistently love people and pray for them often?" Miriam wondered. "We said we need to prepare the soil."

"Yes, that's true," responded Greg, "and I suppose this is related. I guess I'm thinking *how* in the sense of *all at once* or *over time*. I just think we have the tendency to get upset—I know I do—when sharing the gospel with someone if we haven't gotten it all out, the whole gospel on the table. And then, when I do share the whole gospel, they don't respond."

Grabbing the marker and going to the flip chart, Greg continued. "Let's call this style, oh, I don't know … Initial Contact Evangelism." Greg scribbled the words and drew two stick figures.

"Here we are with a person," Greg continued, scribbling as he spoke, "in some kind of initial contact that we either planned or that was an unexpected encounter. We share the gospel *in its entirety*. You know what I mean? We dump the truck! And we challenge the person to make a faith commitment. If the person doesn't trust Christ at that moment, we *may* refocus our evangelistic communication with him or her and share again, but this *event* is over. The emphasis in this style of evangelism is one climactic event in time. We meet. We proclaim. It's over."

"Yes," Bernard started, but stopped when he realized Greg hadn't finished his thought. He was drawing two new stick figures as best he could so that they looked like they were walking together.

"Maybe there is another style of evangelism. Let's call this one Relational Evangelism," Greg continued slowly as he wrote the two words. "Here we also meet a person either by planning or through a divine encounter.

Initial Contact Evangelism: *emphasizes one climactic event in evangelism*

Relational Evangelism: *emphasizes the entire process of evangelism*

6. *Continue to proclaim and teach the gospel, with ongoing appeals for a faith response*

5. *Continue to focus on overcoming the unbeliever's points of gospel resistance*

4. *Continued contacts with the unbeliever where possible*

3. *Refocus evangelistic communication as per the unbeliever's response*

2. **Share the gospel in its entirety with a challenge for faith response**

1. *Establish initial contact through an unexpected or planned encounter*

Initial Contact Evangelism
(emphasizes one climactic point in evangelism)

We are developing a genuine caring friendship through reoccurring contacts

"But now—and Miri, you just reminded us of this truth—we are developing a genuine caring friendship through *reoccurring* contacts.

"We are sowing seeds," Greg said, drawing a new bullet point on the chart and writing, *by appropriately introducing spiritual issues.* "We continue to share more of the gospel in a loving and tactful manner," he added while drawing still another point on the chart.

"Until," Bern jumped in as Greg drew one more point, "we share the Gospel in its entirety."

6. *Continue to share and teach the gospel, with ongoing appeals for a faith response*

5. ***Share the gospel in its entirety in a ripe opportunity and encourage a faith response***

4. *Continue to share more of the gospel in a loving and factual manner*

3. *Sow gospel seeds by appropriately introducing spiritual issues*

2. *Develop a genuine caring friendship through reoccurring contacts*

1. *Establish initial contact through an unexpected or planned encounter*

Relational Evangelism
(emphasizes the entire process of evangelism)

"Yes," agreed Greg, "but this time we share in a ripe opportunity after the soil has been prepared. We encourage a faith commitment because we are confident the listener *understands* and is ready to *embrace* the gospel or at least has the capacity to do so."

"Aha!" exclaimed Diana. "*That* sounds like the parable again."

"That's right," Miri added, "and it's related to our Evangelism and Discipleship Scale."

"And even in this scenario," finished Greg, drawing and writing out still another point on the chart, "we may not see a positive faith response. If that is the case, we continue to share and teach the gospel with ongoing appeals to a faith commitment decision."

"So the emphasis in Initial Contact Evangelism is a onetime climactic moment?" asked Diana.

"Exactly," replied Greg drawing a circle around the first two points on the bottom of the initial contact chart.

Diana responded by rising from her overstuffed chair and taking the marker from her husband, saying, "If you please."

"Certainly, my dear."

Then Diana continued. "And the emphasis in Relational Evangelism is on the entire process." With that she circled the whole process on the relational chart.

"That's what I'm thinking," Greg exclaimed, clapping his hands and bowing in deference to his wife. "That's why I tried to make the stick figures as if they are walking in the Relational part of the chart. The evangelist and the unbeliever are walking down the road of life together. As the evangelist develops a friendship, he is always up front about his faith. He keeps the gospel before him, not pestering but being open, dropping seeds appropriately. And when his friend is ready, he shares the gospel in its entirety and challenges him to respond in faith. What do you think?"

"This is helpful," commented Bernard thoughtfully. After a brief moment he continued: "So the contrast between Initial Contact Evangelism and Relational Evangelism is one climactic event as opposed to the entire process of evangelism. Are you saying that Initial Contact Evangelism is wrong and Relational Evangelism is right?"

"Not necessarily," replied Greg. "But before we decide that, I think we

ought to look in the Bible. Is it even valid to say that these are two approaches to evangelism? Did Paul use one or the other? When did he use them? What about Jesus?

"Let's see if my rambling and drawing, as great as it is"—Greg commented sarcastically—"is even right. I based my thinking on Acts 16 and tried to think through some other passages, but let's be sure. Let's brainstorm and see if we can identify one or the other or both of these approaches in the New Testament."

➤ *For the next hour and a half the four friends worked through the book of Acts trying to determine which approach was used in each instance. As they did so, they were more and more convinced that both approaches were used. We're going to pick up their conversation toward the end to find out what they learned. For now, do the activity below.*

Exercise #6:

At this point, take a moment to pick up your Bible. Leaf through the book of Acts and look for cases when the gospel was shared and people responded. Can you find both approaches, or at least hints that both have been used?

After you do your survey, look at the chart (next page) the team developed to compare your findings. Then write down advantages you see in each approach. Are there any dangers associated with the approaches? After you answer these questions, read on to learn the team's opinions to the same questions.

Evangelism in the book of Acts

Passage	Initial Contact	Relational	Comments
Acts 2:14-41	✓		Preaching, 3,000 accepted message
Acts 3:12–4:4	✓		with healing, many believed, put in prison
Acts 4:8-17	✓		preached before high priest, freed
Acts 10:23-44 Acts11:5-18	✓	✓	preached to Cornelius and crowd
Acts 11:19-23	✓	?	Word proclaimed as they "made their way"
Acts 13:13-52	✓	✓	in synagogue at least 2 Sabbaths, what did they do between Sabbaths?
Acts 14:1-7		✓	not definitive, "considerable time spent there"
Acts 16:13-15	✓	✓	Lydia, one or other or both
Acts 16:16	✓	✓	"many days"
Acts 16:25-40		✓	crisis, deals with question asked
Acts 17:1-9	✓	✓	3 weeks, Sabbaths and in between
Acts 17:10-15	✓	✓	Bereans examined "every day"
Acts 17:16-34	✓	✓	some sneers, wanted to hear more
Acts 18	✓	✓	Corinth, every Sabbath/tentmaker, 18 months investing in lives
Acts 19	✓	✓	Ephesus 3 months in synogogues, 2 years in Hall of Tyrannus

With the full chart before them, Bernard asked, "So can we sum up what we've learned here?"

"Well," Miriam began, "some of the passages are recordings of preaching sessions before large crowds. The entire gospel was presented at one time, and people were challenged to respond. We could say that was Initial Contact Evangelism even though it was a sermon. Sometimes we are not sure if one approach or another was really used. Other cases indicate clearly that people heard the gospel over extended periods of time, which would seem to indicate Relational Evangelism."

"So both approaches were used," Diana thought out loud. "How do we know which to use when? I mean, I read Joe Aldrich's book[6] and was taught in Bible college that I need to develop friendships with people to gain a hearing. Aldrich and my professors emphasized what we are calling Relational Evangelism. If Initial Contact Evangelism is also valid, when is it appropriate?"

"Good question, Honey," Greg replied. "If we go back to Acts 16 and the Philippian jailer, I think we have a good answer. Here is a man who is panicking and ready to kill himself because he thinks the prisoners have escaped and he will be tortured and killed. Paul stops him, assuring him that all the prisoners are still there. Then the man asks, 'Sirs, what must I do to be saved?' Paul takes advantage of the situation and answers the jailer's question with the best news he could ever receive."

Bible Reference:
Acts 16:25-40

"Initial Contact Evangelism is appropriate when we have a short window of opportunity and don't expect to see the person again," Bernard added. "It could be a deathbed experience, a serendipitous meeting on an airplane—that type of thing. It's better when you know the person is ready to hear the gospel, but since this is a onetime opportunity, you try to share all you can. But even on a plane or in any situation that is not dangerous, if the person is way down the scale, it might be better to simply help them understand who God is and trust God to bring someone else into their lives to bring them further up the scale."

> ***Initial Contact Evangelism is appropriate when we have a short window of opportunity and don't expect to see the person again.***

"Why? Because there is the possibility that the hearer will not understand but make some kind of *decision* anyway?" Diana asked. "We talked about this a couple of

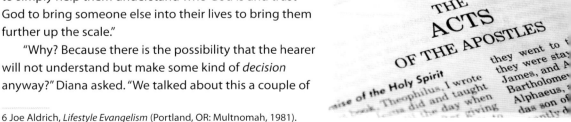

---

6 Joe Aldrich, *Lifestyle Evangelism* (Portland, OR: Multnomah, 1981).

days ago. Berte could have 'prayed to receive Christ' with me just to get me out the door or to bring an end to an uneasy moment."

"Can we take a break?" Miriam asked. "I'd like to check on the kids."

The men looked at each other, each looked at his wife and shrugged their shoulders in unison.

"Sure, why not?" Bernard vocalized his response.

Greg added, "I need to stretch my legs."

Bernard checked his watch and said, "Let's be back in twenty."

How Should We Sow? (Part 2)
Understanding Receptivity

As the group reconvened, Bernard stated, "Just before our break, Diana said she thought Berte could have 'prayed to receive Christ' with her just to get her out the door or to bring an end to a tense moment. That's possible and probably occurs more than we know. But it is equally possible the opposite happens: the hearer *rejects* the gospel because he doesn't fully understand or something in his worldview predisposes him to do so."

"Hold on a second!" interjected Miriam. "What do you mean 'something in his worldview predisposes him to do so'?"

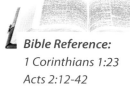

"Well," started Bern, pausing a moment to think, "in 1 Corinthians 1:23 Paul said, 'we preach Christ crucified, a stumbling block to Jews and folly to Gentiles.' The Jews wanted a sign and even though Jesus gave them sign after

Bible Reference:
1 Corinthians 1:23
Acts 2:12-42

sign—the greatest being His resurrection—they stumbled over Him. They weren't seeing it. Their worldview, biblically based but not complete, did not allow for the God-Man so they couldn't—or wouldn't—believe. But when Peter preached on the Day of Pentecost, his listeners were 'cut to the heart' and asked, 'Brothers, what shall we do?' It was then, understanding the gospel more fully, that they responded in faith.

"Now switch scenarios. In Athens when Paul spoke of the Resurrection (Acts 17), some of the Epicurean and Stoic philosophers asked, 'What does this babbler wish to say?' They thought the Resurrection was foolish. These two instances show how a person's worldview can predispose him to reject the gospel. His worldview puts up barriers."

"Mm-hmm," Miriam hummed. "Again, we see the importance of our hearers truly understanding the gospel."

Greg cut in. "This worldview issue may be significant in our presentation of the gospel. We may want to come back to that. But we started this subject when Diana saw the danger in Initial Contact Evangelism of a premature or false decision. Bernard added the possibility of premature rejection of the gospel. We should take note of these significant dangers. Are there any other dangers to this approach?"

A moment of silence reigned. Then Miriam pointed out, "I can see Initial Contact presentations being cold and confrontational although they certainly don't have to be. But it is a possible danger."

"Yes, we should take note of that," agreed Bernard. "I think another danger could be 'dumping the truck' as Greg said. We think we have to share everything, and in our zeal it can be too much, too quickly."

"Dumping the truck" is a possible danger in Initial Contact Evangelism.

"Or it is too confusing for people to grasp all at once," added Greg. "Have you ever been deep into sharing what you think is possibly your best gospel presentation yet and notice this glazed look in your friend's eyes? Oh, how discouraging that is!"

"I know. I've seen that look many times in the eyes of people as you're sharing the gospel, especially in German!" Diana chimed in.

Everyone laughed, knowing they too had seen a glazed look as they plowed on, determined to share the gospel, with or without the attention of their hearers.

"Okay, this is getting a little too close to home—for all of us." Bern winced. "What about Relational Evangelism? What are the advantages of that approach?"

It didn't take long at all for the answers to come.

"We have more time to clearly present the truths of the gospel. We can find out where they are on the E&D Scale and try to 'move them up' in their understanding."

"And they would be hearing this important good news from a friend, not a stranger, which means they might accept it more readily or at least give more consideration to the gospel."

"With Relational Evangelism converts we have more possibility for follow-up and discipleship."

"With Relational Evangelism converts we have more possibility for follow-up and discipleship."

"But certainly there are dangers associated with this approach as well," cautioned Diana. "I know I am reluctant to confront my friends. I am afraid it might end my relationship with them."

"Sure," agreed Greg, "and as a result, we tend not to 'draw the net.' We usually think they are not quite ready."

"Maybe related to that, but a real danger in itself," added Miriam, "is that we might lack a sense of urgency with this approach."

"Oh my, yes," acknowledged Diana. "That's an admonition I remember from friendship evangelism teaching: don't just develop friendships and never get around to sharing the gospel."

"Okay, then," began Bernard in an attempt to recap the morning's work, "Initial Contact and Relational Evangelism are both valid approaches to sharing the gospel, but we want to use them when they are most appropriate and avoid the dangers associated with each." He had been writing comments on the flip chart as they were shared and, pointing to the paper he added, "Does this pretty much sum up what we have said?"

Initial Contact Evangelism

Appropriate:
- Deathbed situations
- When we don't expect to see the person again

Dangers:
- Not understanding
- Premature decisions

Relational Evangelism

Advantages:
- More time, we understand where hearer is on the scale
- More open to hearing from a friend than from a stranger
- More possibility for follow-up

Dangers:
- Don't draw the net
- Reluctant to confront
- Fear of ending relationship

Exercise #7:

Above are Bernard's lists of advantages and dangers. Do you have any thoughts to add?

After everyone agreed, Bernard added, "I'm glad we kept track of those points and summarized them just now. That exercise reminded me of something I thought of last night that I want to include as we work through some of these issues. I once had a teacher who always wanted us to keep track of our *Best Ideas* throughout the class. He said the brain was an amazing thing and ideas, important points, or even epiphanies could come to us at any time. It could be something that he said, something that another student said, or it might just come to us while other things were going on around us. Regardless of where they came from, this teacher insisted we write down these important thoughts so we didn't lose them. He even instructed us to write *My Best Ideas* in the front inside cover of our notebook and record the ideas there. That way, we knew where to go to find and review the most important concepts of the class.

I think we should take time now to think back on what we have learned so far and record our *Best Ideas*. As we move along, we can add to the list."

Bernard ripped off another sheet of paper from the flip chart and wrote "Our Best Ideas" at the top. Then he turned to the others and asked, "Who's first?"

Diana leaned forward eagerly and said, "I like this idea, especially because I don't remember who said it, though I think it was Miri, but just a little bit ago someone mentioned that Relational Evangelism gives more time to clearly present the *truths* of the gospel—not truth, singular, but truths, plural. That really hit me when she said it because it ties in so well with what we discovered as we built the Good Soil Evangelism and Discipleship Scale. So write on the flip chart, 'The gospel is not only *a* truth; it's *many* truths.' Our task is to help people know and understand the truths of the gospel, one by one until they are ready to embrace the gospel."

"Wow!" exclaimed Greg. "That is good. Now I've got a related one for the list. Bern, write 'What can I do with the time I've got? That's all God wants me to do.' The gospel *is* many truths and people need to hear about them and understand them before they can embrace the gospel. I don't have to save people. I can't! I just need to do what

> *"Our task is to help people know and understand the truths of the gospel ..."*

I can to move them up the scale. When someone at minus 11 moves up a notch or two, that's shouting time! We ought to praise God. It's encouraging to know that God can use me to move someone toward Christ and possibly use me again later—or someone else entirely—to bring them even closer."

"Excellent," Bernard responded. "Also in relation to that, I was thinking that the amount of time we spend on any piece of God's overarching story depends on where our listener is on the scale. For example, if my friend understands the biblical concepts of God, man, sin, and death, I need not spend much time there, but can move on to Jesus and the cross. On the other hand, if he is at the bottom of the scale with little understanding of who God is, I need to spend some time there." He paused briefly then asked, "Any other *Best Ideas*, team?"

Miriam looked up from her notes. "As long as we are on the scale, I had an idea this morning as I was looking over what we had learned. Basically we have seen that our task is moving unbelievers up the scale from darkness to light. They start knowing nothing—or little—of the gospel until the light dawns in their hearts. But it occurred to me that maybe the scale is not just one-dimensional; maybe it's at least two. Think with me: moving up the scale is moving from darkness to light, from ignorance to enlightenment as they learn and understand new truths. Can we say they also may need to move from left to right, from being closed to the gospel to being open? We all know people who don't know much about the gospel but are more than willing to hear us out and learn about God. At the same time we know people who know nearly everything there is to know about the gospel and they might be at minus 1 or 2 but are totally closed—you couldn't get them to listen to the gospel if you paid them!"

"So we need not only to get people *up* the scale, but *across* the scale, too?" asked Bernard. "How do we do that?"

"Love, integrity, and time," was the simple response from Miriam. "It's all evangelism—God using people. Part of this whole Relational Evangelism idea is bringing them *across* the scale until they are open to hearing."

"I like that," Greg complimented. "Up and across. As they understand more of the gospel, they move up the scale. As they open up to the gospel, they move across. So," he said as he picked up a marker and began to draw, "we

> "It's encouraging to know that God can use me to move someone toward Christ and possibly use me again later—or someone else entirely—to bring them even closer."

> "Love, integrity, and time."

can add this matrix to our set of Good Soil tools." After a few moments Greg displayed the chart to the team.

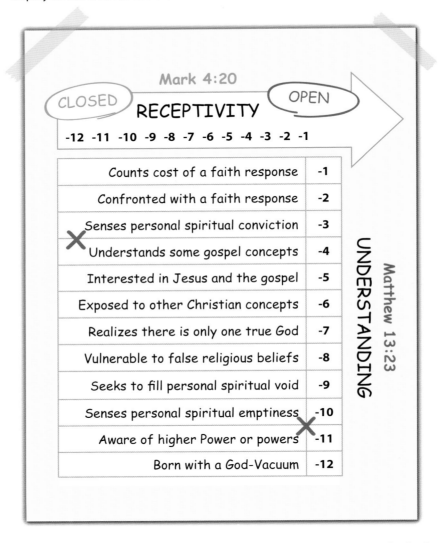

"That's it!" Miriam exclaimed. "That's what I had in mind. We can think of people with whom we are working and place them somewhere within that box. They could know very little of the gospel but be open to hearing." She placed a red *X* in the box, low and to the right.

"Or our friend could know a lot about the gospel, but not be willing to listen," Miriam added as she made a blue *X*. "Or our friends could be anywhere on this matrix. It's our responsibility to live with integrity and love them with such intensity that they open up to hear the gospel. Then we share with them so they understand the gospel."

"I like that." Diana applauded her friend. "I have another *best idea* to add."

"Let's hear it," Bern encouraged.

"Our Good Soil E&D Scale ought not to be understood as if everyone will rigidly move through each point," she answered. "It seems to me that as people hear the gospel and see Jesus in our lives they could jump up—even skip points—in the chart. Each and every point does not have to be touched on as you would step up a staircase."

"No, they could skip over some just like I take steps two or three at a time!" Greg exclaimed. "I think you're right, though. The points on the scale are to be taken as generally true about all of us. Mankind begins at the bottom and needs to move from the unknown to the known as is illustrated in the scale. Hear, hear."

"I agree."

"Yes, we need to be careful," came the other responses.

"Well, we've got a good *Best Ideas* list here," Bern noticed. "The kids will be getting hungry, and I know my stomach is growling a bit. I have one more item I've been thinking about. Let's see if you can help me phrase it in such a way that we can get it on the list, and then break for lunch. Here goes. Even though I believe the Holy Spirit regenerates a person at a specific point in time, it appears there is a process involved here. Could we call it a conversion process? I'm speaking of the time it takes for someone to move along up—or across—the scale. Some hear the gospel and trust Christ in a very short time, within minutes of hearing! Others may have their core

Our Best Ideas

1. The gospel is not only a truth; it is many truths.

2. What can I do with the time I have? That is all God wants me to do.

3. The time we spend on each piece of God's story depends on where the unbeliever is on the scale.

4. Our task is moving unbelievers up the scale from darkness to light.

5. Love, integrity, and time help move unbelievers "across" the scale from being closed to open to the gospel.

6. The scale is not to be understood as people having to move rigidly through each point or even in the same order.

7. The conversion of unbelievers can be a gradual process that leads to the instantaneous point of regeneration.

Exercise #8:

Do you have any "Best Ideas" to add to this list?

worldview beliefs challenged bit by bit over time. So their conversion is not instantaneous, but a process."

Bernard could tell his colleagues were getting nervous with his language so he quickly added, "Hear me out. We've said that the points on the Evangelism and Discipleship Scale all represent understandings—about God, about the Bible, about themselves, and Christ—which people must come to have before they place their trust in Christ, right? Well, let's look at some examples to help bring some light to this conversion/regeneration discussion."

Pointing to the bottom of the scale and sliding his finger up to -7, Bernard

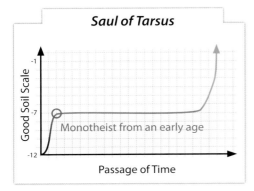

Saul of Tarsus

Good Soil Scale

-1

-7 ⊙ Monotheist from an early age

-12

Passage of Time

continued, "Saul of Tarsus would have moved up to -7 early in life as he was reared by his Jewish parents, studied the Torah, and went to the synagogue. He probably became a monotheist quite naturally within the first four to seven years of his life. His culture influenced him that way. But when faced with Christianity, he fought it for some time until his Damascus road encounter. Apparently, such a dramatic confrontation and the soul-searching it produced moved him up the scale to the point of placing his faith in Jesus as Messiah in just a few days or even hours.

"Now think about …" Bernard paused briefly to think, then continued with, "Cornelius. This Roman soldier's upbringing would have made him a polytheist who worshipped idols. Yet, over time (we don't know how much time), the Holy Spirit used events and people in his life, and possibly the Old Testament Scriptures, to bring him to the point of being a monotheist. In Acts 10:2 we see he was a 'devout man who feared God.' So over time, Cornelius"—

Bible Reference:
Acts 10:2

as Bernard spoke, he moved his hand up the scale to -7—"was converted to a monotheist. Then, when Peter spoke to Cornelius and the group gathered in his home, he moved up farther to the point of trusting Christ as savior. We don't know how long it took him to move to -7; it could have been years. But in his case, he moved the next 7 steps in a matter of hours or minutes. Part of his conversion may have taken years, part of it took less time."

Cornelius

Good Soil Scale

-1

-7 Monotheist prior to meeting Peter ⊙

-12

Passage of Time

"Hmm," Greg responded, "I think I'm understanding your point. Lydia, too (from Acts 16), moved up the

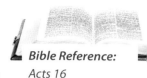

scale to monotheism over time. We know this because she was at the river-side place of prayer. Then, when confronted with the gospel of Christ—in one session or several—the conversion process continued. We don't know if she took a longer or shorter time than Cornelius to move up the scale, but to illustrate the fact that people respond differently, let's show her path as more gradual."

Bible Reference:
Acts 16

"But the jailer," Miri jumped into the conversation, "appears to have moved quickly from pagan to believer in just a few minutes or hours."

"That's right," Bern answered, smiling. It looked like everyone was catching on. "Maybe it was the dramatic crisis in his life or maybe he had given it some thought before, but the only deduction we can make from the evidence we have from the story is that his conversion was almost as *instantaneous* as his regeneration. The point I'm trying to make is that conversion is a process that leads to the point of regeneration."

"So what you're saying is that people are changing their minds about important issues—they are *converting*—over time until the Holy Spirit regenerates them?" Diana asked.

"Yes, the conversion process may be long or short, but it is a process. Make sense to everybody?"

"Very much so," Greg responded. "And what an encouragement it is for intensive prayer and the teaching of God's Word—especially as it relates to the Holy Spirit using it and our efforts in the lives of unbelievers as we patiently work and watch Him work over time."

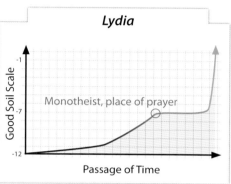

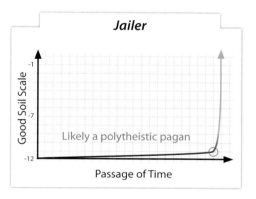

"Yes, the Holy Spirit uses God's Word to change lives as we faithfully teach it," added Miriam. "Even though it takes time, it is well worth our effort if we will just trust God to do the work of changing hearts and lives."

Diana, holding back tears, spoke up. "This morning Kaylie asked if we really had to leave tomorrow. The kids have been having so much fun that they want to stay. Now it's my turn to ask, 'Do we have to leave?'" She wiped her eyes and her nose and then continued. "I am learning so much as we work together." More sniffles. A pause as she gained composure. "I don't want

to leave either. Only it's more than that." Another pause. "I don't want to leave Germany! You two …" She had to stop again, then continued. "You two and your family are so dear to us, and we learn so much from each other, and …"

During this pause, Miri moved to put her arm around her. Bern Looked at Greg to determine what to do next and saw his buddy was also having difficulty staying composed. He was about to suggest they pray when Diana tried again.

"We've learned so much already, and we can continue to study, and …" She pulled in a few short sniffles, but she kept going. "And if we work hard at doing what we're learning about evangelism, can't we stay?" Diana finished and turned to look at Greg.

The question hung in the air a long moment. Greg was feeling the same emotions as Diana, but he did not want to make a rash, emotional decision. *Sure, we are learning together,* he thought. *And what we are learning are powerful, significant truths—the type of thing that pastors and missionaries wish they had been taught in seminary. I believe the application of the insights we are gaining could very well change the course of our ministry whether it would be in Germany or anywhere else in the world! But …*

He couldn't answer because he couldn't even finish his thoughts in his own head. Bern saw the struggle in his friend's eyes and bowed his head to pray. He started slowly, falteringly, but gained strength as the Holy Spirit guided him. He was truly leading in prayer; all hearts in the room were following and agreeing, pleading with the Lord for wisdom, placing their trust in Him for direction and comfort.

During the prayer hearts were calmed. When Bern closed with "Amen" not a word was necessary. Greg and Diana embraced and headed off to get the kids for lunch. Bern and Miri tided up and headed downstairs as well.

Diana understood Greg's hesitancy. She knew this was something they had been struggling with for a long time. As they walked down the long semi-circular stairway, she acknowledged the fact that it would take time or clear direction from God to move him.

As she gave him a squeeze around the waist, she thought, *I can depend upon the Lord for His guidance and His timing. It might take quite awhile for you to be sure. Or it could be today.*

"Let it be today," she prayed silently as they caught sight of the kids and smiled.

Part Two

HELPING *UNBELIEVERS*
UNDERSTAND

the Gospel

What Do They Hear?
Why Unbelievers Don't Understand the Gospel

Lunchtime was filled with the kids' reports on their adventures in the water park that morning.

"You should have seen …"

"And then I …"

"… the biggest belly flop ever!"

The adults listened with pleasure, trying to get the tales straight as the animated storytellers bounced from one event to the other and back again, stopping only to stuff another bite into their mouths. "Don't talk with your mouth full" was a forgotten admonition in the midst of so much excitement.

None of the children seemed to notice that Greg was preoccupied, for which he was grateful. He didn't see the need to rain on their parade, especially on the last day of the retreat.

He agreed with Diana. He really did. But this wasn't a situation where he could just say, "Oh, we missed a couple of things that we figured out this weekend. Now that we've got it fixed, everything is okay." He wanted to stay in Germany, too—he never really wanted to leave! But they had struggled through the decision-making process, had it set, and now the conflict was back.

The problem was he knew Diana was right; they all were right. The truths they had discovered over the past two days could make a real difference if they applied them in their ministry. But it still would be difficult. And that's what truly was bothering him.

Notwithstanding, he thought to himself as his middle daughter told her story about the "curlicue" slide for the third time, *the knowledge of the necessity of making authentic disciples through long-term relationships, of not just sharing information but building trust relationships, and of the need to listen to our hearers, being hearers ourselves and not "tellers"—these key concepts will help enable us to do the difficult.*

… making authentic disciples through long-term relationships … building trust relationships …

Actually Greg was almost as ready to recommit to a lifetime of making disciples in Germany as Diana appeared to be. It didn't matter that he had already told Joe Shepherd (their boss, the European Administrator of the mission) that they were strongly considering leaving. Joe had tried to talk him out of it last week after Greg told him of his plans to break the news to Bernard and Miriam at this retreat and ask them to take their place in the tiny ministry. But at that time Greg had been firm. "Diana and I have spent time praying and talking through this, Joe," Greg said on the international call. "We don't want to waste money people have given sacrificially for the Lord's work if we're not being effective." Joe gave him the usual arguments about the work being slow and difficult in Western Europe, but Greg didn't budge.

Now, however, Greg was sensing their recent study was equipping them to do the task he believed God had called them to do in Germany. *In fact,* Greg thought, *slowing down the process and ramping up the biblical information as we build relationships should be our approach to sharing the gospel in Germany, America, or anywhere in the world.* He just wanted to be sure about Germany and be done with the waffling. *Let's just see what this afternoon's study brings*, he thought. *Then I'll decide.*

> **Slowing down the process and ramping up the biblical information as we build relationships should be our approach to sharing the gospel … anywhere in the world.**

The thought had barely passed through his mind, and Greg checked himself. *What am I thinking, Lord?* he prayed silently. *I sound so selfish. This is not my "decision" to make. This is Your work, Your calling. Teach us through this afternoon's study, Lord, and help me respond to Your leading. God, I pray that You will teach us and equip us to serve You and be effective for You here in Germany or wherever you lead us.*

💬 *This is Your work, Your calling. Teach us … equip us to serve You and be effective …*

With Allie on her shoulder, Amber led Bernard and Miriam back to the Sämanns' apartment with the other kids in tow. That was where the

Monopoly® game was to be played right after their afternoon naps. Since the group was planning on going to the Mexican restaurant on this their last evening, both sets of parents insisted all the children at least lie down for a while. After the usual groans and weak complaints the kids felt they needed to try on their folks, they agreed. Enjoying Mexican food in Germany did not happen often, so they were excited and would "endure" a nap.

Amber smiled as she went. She planned to read to them, watch as they nodded off one by one, and then get a little shut-eye as well.

A few minutes later Greg and Diana locked the door to their apartment and headed to the meeting place in silence, holding hands. Diana spoke first. "You were pretty quiet at lunch. Is everything all right?"

"Actually, everything is great. In my wildest dreams I could not have anticipated the significance of this retreat. Of course, it's going in a completely different direction than I expected, but that's what is making it so important. Instead of us telling the Sämanns we're leaving and developing a transition plan, we've come across—no, I believe God has enabled us to learn—some invaluable insights."

"I agree," Diana responded softly.

"I'm sorry to have left you hanging there before lunch, Sweetie," Greg apologized, trailing off. He wanted to say more, to let her know that she was not the problem, it was he who was acting silly and that he was so close, but he wasn't quite sure what to say.

Diana just squeezed his hand and then stopped walking. Since she was holding tight to Greg's hand, her stop pulled him up short. Greg turned to look at her. Diana, with eyes about to overflow, smiled and looked into his eyes. "I know you'll make the right decision, and I will accept it and support you in it whatever it is. I believe you desire to serve faithfully the God you love and to do His will. I am so glad I married you."

Greg enveloped her in his arms and lifted her off the ground in a huge bear hug. He couldn't count the number of times he had realized what a gift God had given him in Diana. At those times he would turn to her and say, "I'm glad I married you, Diana." Then she would blush or smile or give him a peck on the cheek, so he could tell she appreciated it. But she had never responded with, "I'm glad I married *you*, Greg." After thirteen years of marriage she had chosen this moment to affirm him with "his" phrase. He felt he was going to burst with happiness and gratitude to God.

And he felt he could do anything God asked of him.

The two couples ended up reaching the meeting place at the same time. Bernard thought Greg looked unusually cheerful considering he had left the last session so downcast. Miriam slipped over to Diana to give her a squeeze around the waist. The two spoke softly to each other for a moment.

Then Bernard started the final meeting by reviewing the subjects they had discussed, pointing to and reading the appropriate flip chart sheet for each:

- *Parable of the Soils*, including the significant verbs that describe the *good soil* person who understands, embraces, and retains the Word
- *Good Soil Evangelism and Discipleship Scale* with its list of human responses through which hearers must move in order to come to and grow in Christ, along with the three stages of evangelism they called tilling, planting, and reaping
- *Eight essential Gospel elements* they had defined: God, man, sin, death, Christ, cross, faith, life
- *Initial Contact Evangelism versus Relational Evangelism*
- *Understanding-Receptivity Matrix* revealing our need to "love people to Christ" or help them move "across the scale" from closed to open

"Now," Bernard continued after the review, "eventually we may want to spend more time with each of these evangelism-defining words from the parable of the sower. For example, I'd like to think we could develop our theology/philosophy of evangelism by working on each of these challenges:

- "Helping *Unbelievers* Understand the Gospel"
- "Helping *Unbelievers* Embrace the Gospel"
- "Helping *Believers* Retain the Gospel"

If these three concepts—unbelievers definitely need to understand the gospel before they can make a faith response, unbelievers then need to truly embrace the gospel, and true believers retain the gospel—are as important as we think they are, then they certainly merit our careful study and the development of skills to put them into practice."

Everyone nodded assent without speaking a word. Although Bernard would have liked a commitment from everyone to continue their studies together after the retreat, he decided now was not the time to push for it, so he pressed on.

"With the time remaining today, I'd like at least to think about how we can help unbelievers understand the gospel." Pointing to the large sheet of paper from two days ago, Bernard continued, "Remember the Greek word *suniemi* means 'to comprehend, mentally grasp, or see how it all fits together.' Good soil hearers comprehend the gospel. So one of our major objectives should be to help unbelievers understand the gospel! I have a question to get us started: Why?"

"What do you mean?" Greg queried.

"Well, we know that unbelievers who are *good soil* do understand because Jesus stated that they understand. But others—and there are a boatload of them—*don't*. So the question is why don't unbelievers understand the gospel?"

"Why don't unbelievers understand the gospel?"

"Hmm. The answer is simple: spiritual blindness," Greg answered matter-of-factly. "Paul wrote about this in 2 Corinthians 4:3-4, 'And even if our gospel is veiled, it is veiled to those who are perishing. In their case the god of this world has blinded the minds of the unbelievers, to keep them from seeing the light of the gospel of the glory of Christ, who is the image of God.'"

Bible Reference:
2 Corinthians 4:3-4

"Right!" shouted Bernard. "And that is true of *all* unbelievers to the same degree until the Holy Spirit opens their eyes. But I think there is another reason why unbelievers don't understand the gospel. This one varies greatly from person to person."

"Is this going to be related to that 'worldview thing' you mentioned this morning?" asked Miriam.

Bernard shot a surprised glance at his wife. "How did you know?"

"Well, you used the examples of Paul in Jerusalem and Athens to illustrate how a person's worldview can predispose him to reject the gospel or at least put up barriers that we need to get past."

"That's right," complimented Bernard. "I'm impressed by your memory."

"I had a great teacher," Miriam raved.

"Anyway," Bernard, now bright red, responded sheepishly, "help me out here." As he continued to talk, he drew a man holding a Bible and talking to another person on the flip chart. "Let's say I want to share the gospel with someone. Before I can do that I have to have an idea of what the gospel is. How do we want to summarize the gospel on our chart?"

"*Johannes 3:16,*" Miriam answered.

"All right, good," Bernard acknowledged as he wrote "My understanding of the meaning of John 3:16" in a cartoon bubble above the first person's head. "But you realize that I have a somewhat biblical worldview. My understanding of the world is shaped by the Bible. I believe it is God's Word, therefore, what it tells me about God and the world and all that is in it, I take to be true. So my understanding of John 3:16, I hope, reflects a biblical worldview. Someone else's *meaning* of John 3:16 may be skewed by their worldview."

1. Understand
My understanding of the meaning of John 3:16.

"Huh?" interrupted Miriam. "I think I understood everything you said, but I'm not sure what all the fuss is about. My meaning, your meaning, what does all that *mean*?" she asked, a bit of irony in her voice.

"Well," Bernard started, thinking and then chuckling. "This might be a good illustration. Remember that drug addict I was talking with three or four weeks ago? If I were to say Paul was 'stoned in Lystra,' those words could create a completely different image in his mind. Unbiblical elements exist in his worldview that confuse his understanding of those words."

Giggles, chuckles, and then laughter grew among the group as the meaning of "stoned" for the drug addict sunk in for each of them. Then Bernard continued.

"So now I know *what* I need to communicate with my friend. I have the meaning of the gospel in my head. What is the next step I need to take?"

The room was quiet as the friends thought about the question, the kind of silence experienced in classrooms when teachers ask questions that require obvious answers that no one wants to give.

Unbiblical elements exist in his worldview that confuse his understanding of those words.

Finally Diana hazarded a response. "You tell your friend the gospel."

"Okay, thank you, Diana. That certainly is about to happen, but I'd like to put another step in here first," Bernard responded as he wrote the number one in the original cartoon bubble and drew a second callout with the number two inside. "Since I have plenty of options to communicate the good news of Jesus Christ with people, let's say that next I will encode my message. All I'm saying is that once I decide I will share the gospel with my friend, I then need to decide in what format I will present it. Maybe I will talk to him personally, maybe I will give him a gospel tract, maybe I will use visuals, maybe I'll invite him to one of our special events at church, or maybe I will use a combination of methods. But the fact is that first I choose to encode my message—put it into one format or another.

1. Understand
My understanding of the meaning of John 3:16.

2. Encode

3. Transmit

"Then," Bernard continued, writing the number three and the word "Transmit" over an arrow on the paper, "I transmit my message to my friend in the most appropriate means for the format I have chosen. For example, if I have encoded the message orally, I will transmit it by speaking. If I have chosen to use written words, I hand my friend a book or tract."

Greg had stayed quiet, but he was getting excited as the discussion went on and the illustration was being built. If this discussion was going the direction he thought, it could have significant ramifications for sharing the gospel in Germany, or anywhere else in the world. He waited patiently as Bernard continued.

Worldview noise: the effect of the unbiblical elements in one's worldview belief system that confuse his understanding of gospel truths and/or predispose him to reject the gospel.

"Now if my friend, the gospel recipient, has a worldview that differs from a biblical worldview," Bernard spoke as he wrote, "that message is going to be somewhat confused by, let's call it, 'worldview noise.' In any communication process, 'noise' is anything that hinders a clear understanding of the message from presenter to recipient." With that Bernard scribbled over the transmitting line to illustrate noise.

Miriam interrupted with, "When I talk with my mother in Austria over the Internet, we sometimes have static that keeps us from understanding each other."

"Exactly," Bernard agreed. "That interference 'noise' confuses the conversation. Worldview noise can be just as disappointing—more so—because it confuses my message to my friend here."

With that Greg jumped up and approached Bernard. "May I have the marker?" he asked with a smile. Bernard, seeing the twinkle in Greg's eye, just grinned, handed him the marker, and stepped aside.

"I think I know where you are going with this," Greg bubbled. He quickly drew a callout above the recipient's head. Then pointing at it, he ventured, "Our desire in this communication process is for Bernard's friend to get the true meaning of the gospel." Greg stopped talking long enough to write *The true meaning of John 3:16* in the callout. "But before he can arrive there he first has to decode the message; he has to make sense of it." On the end of the arrow closest to the recipient he wrote *Decode*. "But," Greg continued, "the accuracy of his decoding, that is, the degree to which he understands the message Bernard wants to communicate, will be affected significantly by the density of the worldview noise." With this, Greg scribbled even more over the communication line between the two friends. "The greater the difference between the recipient's worldview and a biblical worldview, the more dense the worldview noise will be and hence, the greater possibility for not understanding. Bernard's friend *could* end up with something completely different in his callout!"

With that Greg wrote something that resembled gibberish in the recipient's callout, illustrating the lack of understanding.

"So let me see if I get what you're saying," Miriam ventured. "Even though Bernard understands the gospel and gives what he would consider a clear presentation of the gospel, his friend may not get it because something in the way he looks at the world skews his understanding. Is that right?"

"That's it," Bernard replied. "What about you, Diana? Does this make sense to you?"

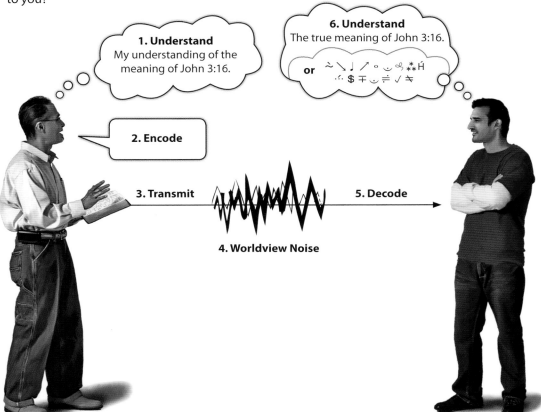

Is That So Bad?
Negative Effects of Misunderstanding the Gospel

"I think I understand," Diana answered Bernard's question hesitantly. "Can you give me a real live example? And not just the drug addict story."

"Um, sure," Bernard responded. "Let's say I tell my friend, 'God loves you.' Simple enough, right? And my friend says, 'That's great. Which one of the more than 330 million gods and goddesses are you talking about?' His Hindu worldview has put up a barrier to the gospel."

"Oh, I see," Diana rejoined. "You mentioned the possibility of negative results because of worldview noise. Could we come up with some of those?"

"That's an excellent idea, Diana," Bernard congratulated. "However, it must be clear that the problem isn't so much the unbiblical worldview of our friend that is at issue, but *our understanding*, or lack of it, of his worldview and the realization that we must cut through his worldview noise."

"So are we saying we need to know the worldview of our audience before we share the gospel?" Greg ventured.

"What do you think, gang?" Bernard shot the ball back in their court.

"Hmm."

"Yeah, I guess."

"I believe so."

"I agree," Bernard concurred, "which means we are going to have to figure out how to do that. But first, let's go back to Diana's suggestion." He turned to the easel, flipped to a clean sheet of paper and wrote, "Possible Negative Results of Not Cutting through World-view Noise." Then he challenged, "Let's brainstorm. What are some of these negative results?"

> *… the problem isn't so much the unbiblical worldview of our friend … but our understanding, or lack of it, of his worldview …*

Exercise #9:

Complete this exercise before turning the page. Make a list of negative results you may see if you do not understand and effectively cut through worldview noise. Have you personally experienced any of these? Please explain.

"Well," Greg started, "if we use words that have multiple meanings without defining or explaining the words, we'll just confuse our hearers."

"Or we could offend them unintentionally," added Miriam.

"And with undefined terms, people could just think we are crazy!" exclaimed Diana.

"I'm used to that," joked Greg. "Just opening my mouth as I buy groceries or go to the post office draws strange looks from people." Greg paused as everyone laughed. "On a more serious note, though, I could deceive myself."

"What do you mean?" asked Miriam as Bernard added another observation to the sheet.

> *If I don't understand my audience's worldview, I could be deceiving myself. I walk away thinking I've shared the gospel, but my audience isn't any closer to faith because I haven't really communicated.*

"Well, I'm spouting off gospel truths one after the other, thinking I've got my audience spellbound, when in reality they aren't getting it. The barriers put up by their worldview may be confusing or offending them or whatever. I walk away thinking I've shared the gospel. I've done my job. But I'm just deceiving myself. My audience isn't any closer to faith because I haven't really communicated."

"Ouch!" Bernard took in the gravity of Greg's conclusion. After a pensive pause, he added, "This deceiving of ourselves is even more severe when it is linked to a result I wanted to add: false professions. If we don't understand potential worldview noise and counteract it, we could easily see false professions of faith, right?"

"Sure."

"And if we don't realize what's going on," Bernard continued, we could deceive ourselves, thinking people are coming to the Lord."

"And what about syncretism? You know, blending different systems of belief?" Diana contributed.

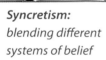

Syncretism:
*blending different
systems of belief*

"Oh my, yes," agreed Miriam. "If we say, 'believe on the Lord Jesus Christ' without establishing the uniqueness of God, a person who believes in many gods could say, 'I believe.' We think he is 'saved,' but the truth of the matter is the person has just put Jesus on the shelf right next to his other gods. He simply added this new information we gave him into his already existing belief system."

"Another possible result is that we could put our hearers back a few steps in their coming to faith," added Greg. "If we don't understand our audience and use language that communicates *to them*, we may inadvertently push people *back down* the scale."

"And getting them back up may prove difficult," warned Bernard. "This may be exactly the type of thing the writer of Hebrews cautioned against in chapter six." He thumbed to Hebrews in his Bible. "Now I know this is a controversial passage, but it seems to relate to the rocky soil, where the hearer receives the Word with joy, but having no root, falls away. The writer of Hebrews warns in verses 4 to 6 that 'it is impossible, in the case of those who have once been enlightened … and then have fallen away, to restore them again to repentance.'

Bible Reference:
Hebrews 6:4-6

"We know that real *good soil* disciples truly understand, embrace, and retain the gospel. But until they get to that point, the rocky soil example and Hebrews 6 tell us that it is difficult to be close, move backward, and then forward again."

"Impossible even," Miriam added ominously.

The room was quiet except for the faint sound of sliders and swimmers on the other side of the thick glass. The group realized that the necessity of cutting through worldview noise was serious business.

"Well, you have come up with some great observations here," Bernard concluded. "I only have one more that I wanted to share: missed opportunities. I was just thinking that when we don't understand our hearer's worldview, we could end up missing opportunities to lovingly address unbiblical worldview issues as a prelude to the gospel. Maybe this could be seen as reverse worldview noise," he continued chuckling. "My friend could say something that reveals a piece of his unbiblical worldview, but because it is just noise to me, I let it go and miss an opening for the gospel."

"We have a missionary friend in Papua New Guinea that might be an example of this," Diana added. "When he got to the field he learned about some unusual nuances of the culture. If he had thought of the strange things he was learning as just 'noise,' he would have missed an unprecedented opportunity to understand the people. Instead, he took down all of the new information, studied it, and was able to share the gospel more clearly with his host culture when the time came."

"Wow, these are great insights," Greg commented. "I'm not sure what we can do about all this, but these are definitely potential dangers and opportunities we face in the gospel communication process. Could we stop to pray?"

Here is the group's list. Compare yours to it and add any insights they may have missed. ➡

Possible Negative Results of Not Cutting through Worldview Noise:

- Confusion
- Offense
- People think we are crazy
- Deceive self (thinking the content I shared is fine)
- False professions
- Syncretism
- Put people back a few steps (down the scale)
- Getting back (closer to faith) may be difficult
- Missed opportunities for sharing the gospel
-
-
-

"Good idea," agreed Bernard. "Let's ask God for wisdom in understanding and cutting through worldview noise."

After their prayer time the two couples took a short break to stretch and check on Amber and the kids. The ladies let them know that in two hours they would be loading the vans and heading to the Mexican restaurant for their last meal in Kaiserslautern. In the morning they would get up and out early, eating breakfast along the way. Amber planned the kids' remaining time, allowing for showers and getting dressed for dinner.

When the couples reconvened for their final session of the retreat, they studied three passages in which the gospel presenters shared with people of distinctly different worldviews. They wanted to see if the presentations of the gospel reflected the worldview differences of the hearers or not.

Bernard pulled two sheets off the flip chart and taped them to the wall on either side of the chart. Then he wrote "Jews" on the sheet on the left, "Lystran Pagans" on the flip chart sheet, and "Epicureans & Stoics" on the right-hand sheet. "Now that we have read these passages," he began, "let's compare and contrast them. Very quickly we can see that the Jews of Acts 2 have some advantages over the other two groups—and most people groups in the world—as to where they start on the E&D Scale. They were *God-fearing Jews* (verse 5) and *converts to Judaism* (verse 11). These *men of Israel*, as Peter calls them in verse 22, have already moved up the scale significantly because of the teaching they received since they were children. So here is probably the first comparison question we should ask: Of the eight essential gospel concepts (God, man, sin, death, Christ, cross, faith, life), which of these did the Jews already understand fairly well?"

Exercise #10:

To better understand their discussion, please read the Bible passages listed below.

Bible References:

Acts 2:5-41

Acts 14:6-18

Acts 17:16-34

"Well, the Torah emphasizes the uniqueness of God," Diana responded.

"And tells how He created man as a responsible being," added Miriam.

"Yes, and the Jews would have had a pretty good understanding of man's choice to disobey God and the consequence of sin that brought death," Greg contributed.

Jews

Where on the Scale?

-4 to -7

Advantages?

Knew God of the Bible and had the Word of God

Understood which of the 8 gospel concepts?

God, Man, Sin, Death

Where did Peter begin to witness and why?

With Christ because that is the next essential gospel element chronologically

"So really," Bernard summarized, "they probably understood the first four points quite well. On the E&D Scale then, Peter's audience was somewhere between -7 and -4, right?"

All agreed.

Bernard continued, "The next question is with which gospel concept could Peter begin to witness, and why?"

"In verse 22 he said, 'Men of Israel, hear these words: Jesus of Nazareth …' He started with Christ," Greg answered.

"He dealt with His deity, death on the cross, and resurrection," Miriam listed as she looked down through the verses.

"So since the Jews had a good understanding of God, man, sin, and death, Peter started his witness with Christ," summarized Bernard. "That's the next essential gospel element chronologically.

"Now let's compare this with how Paul dealt with the pagan worldview culture in Lystra. Turn to Acts 14 to review what we read. Where do you think people in this Lystran crowd were on the Good Soil E&D Scale when Paul began to preach to them?"

Bible Reference:
Acts 14:15

Miriam began, "We don't get to read Paul's message until we get to verse 15. Apparently, early in Paul's presentation, people wanted to offer sacrifices to Paul and Barnabas as if they were gods! Paul healed a crippled man, and the people thought he was Hermes and Barnabas was Zeus. Talk about a different culture! Why would they think that? I mean, I understand a miracle was performed and people attributed it to gods or supernatural beings they worshipped. But why did they think Paul and Barnabas were specifically Hermes and Zeus? Why not any other ancient Greek gods? I guess I don't know too much about Greek and Roman mythology."

"I don't know a lot about it either," Bernard admitted. "But I do remember something I learned in seminary.

I think it was an old Roman poet who told of a previous visit by Zeus and Hermes to this region. They came in human form visiting one thousand homes, but no one showed them hospitality except for one poor elderly couple. Since they invited the gods into their home, this man and wife were the only ones spared when the gods flooded the valley and destroyed its inhabitants. The couple's shack was transformed into a marble-pillared, gold-roofed temple and they became its priests."[7]

"Wow!" Greg exclaimed. "I never heard that. That explains so much. These people knew that story and didn't want to miss an opportunity again, so they began the sacrifices right away. I noticed that the people said 'The gods have come down to us in the likeness of men!' *in the Lycaonian language.* Paul and Barnabas may not have understood what was happening at first if they didn't know the language. They may have thought, 'Wow, look at this positive response! Isn't this great?' It was only later as they realized what was going on that they tore their clothes in grief. What a great example of worldview noise! Not only did the people not 'get it' at first, but Paul and Barnabas could have been deceived into thinking that there was a great response."

"So where were the people in this Lystran crowd on the Good Soil E&D Scale when Paul began preaching to them?" Bernard asked.

"They certainly didn't understand who God is," Diana responded. "I imagine they would have been somewhere around -8 to -11."

"I think you're right," agreed Bernard. "And you've answered our next question, too. They probably didn't understand any of the eight essential gospel concepts. So with which of the concepts did Paul begin to explain the gospel once he encountered the worldview noise?"

Miriam responded this time. "In verse 15 Paul cries out, 'why are you doing these things? We also are men, of like nature with you, and we bring you good news, that you should turn from these vain things to a living God, who made the heaven and the earth and the sea and all that is in them.' Paul started with God the creator."

"Yes, and what a different first step from Peter's in Acts 2," Greg commented. "This is significant material, Bern."

"Preach it!" Bernard cheered Greg on. "This is something we haven't done that could change the way we

---

Lystran/Pagans

Where on the Scale?

-8 to -11

Understood which of the 8 gospel concepts?

None

Where did Paul begin to witness and why?

With God and Man because they believed Greek mythology and wanted to worship Paul and Barnabas

---

7 William J. Larkin Jr., The IVP NT Commentary Series, *Acts*, p 212-13.

evangelize. But here's another question: What did Paul say to challenge and correct their faulty worldview concepts?"

Greg answered again, "Since he was challenging their perception of Barnabas and Paul as gods, he affirmed that they were 'men with the same nature as you' and then went on to preach about God as creator."

"Good," Bernard answered, filling in the chart, then guided the group to the final passage. "Now let's see how the group in Athens compares to the other two. Flip over to chapter 17. Where do you think the Athenians were on the Good Soil E&D Scale when Paul *began* evangelizing?"

Bible Reference:
Acts 17:17-24

"Well, verse 17 says that Paul reasoned in the synagogue with some Jews and God-fearing Greeks. However, Paul's message recorded in Acts 17 is delivered to Epicurean and Stoic philosophers starting with verse 18," Greg responded. "But they weren't too impressed with what he had to say! They called him a 'babbler' and reasoned that he was advocating foreign gods."

"But what do, or did, these philosophers believe?" asked Diana. "I don't have a clue. And without knowing what they believe, I can't place them on the scale."

"Whew, that's a big question with a potentially bigger answer," Miriam responded. She had been a philosophy major. "In some ways they opposed each other. Hmm."

Miriam stopped for a moment to think how best to summarize the two belief systems. Then she continued. "Both worldviews are materialistic in nature, meaning the only thing that can be truly proven to *exist* is *matter*. This led Epicurus to disbelieve in the existence of gods, or at least in the intervention of gods if they existed. Stoics, however, believed that a divine reality pervades the universe, meaning pantheism—god is in everything. For Epicureans pleasure reigns supreme; the highest goal in life is to pursue pleasure, albeit simple pleasures. Stoics believed that human souls will perish; there is no immortality, so 'going with the flow' or keeping your will in accord with nature would bring happiness and thus should be pursued."

Pantheism:
god is in everything

"*Danke, Liebling,*" Bernard acknowledged his wife's contribution. Then he addressed the group. "So based on what we learned about Epicureans and Stoics, from Miriam, as well as what we have read in Acts 17, where do you think Paul's hearers were on the Good Soil E&D Scale when he began evangelizing and which of the gospel concepts did they understand fairly well?"

"Without a belief in God, were they as low as -11 or -12?" asked Diana, tenuous still on her understanding of these worldviews. "And I would guess they didn't have any biblical understanding of the gospel concepts."

"And I would guess you are right, Di," Bernard encouraged. "So did you notice with which of the eight gospel concepts Paul began to witness? Look at verse 18."

"He was preaching about Jesus," answered Miriam.

"That's right, and this is the section Greg was talking about," Bernard stated, becoming intense. "They wondered what this 'babbler' was 'wishing to say' and remarked, 'He seems to be a preacher of foreign divinities.' Look at the end of that verse. They said this, "because he was preaching Jesus and the resurrection.' We mentioned 1 Corinthians 1:23 before, that Paul preached 'Christ crucified: … folly to Gentiles.' It was foolishness because their world-view was so different and didn't allow for what Paul shared. But Paul shifted gears, didn't he? After calling him a babbler and calling his ideas strange in verse 20, they asked Paul to clear things up for them, because after all in verse 21, they liked spending 'their time in nothing except telling or hearing something new.' So now Paul starts with the 'God who made the world and everything in it …' in verse 24. I like this passage because it shows that when Paul realized the worldview and lack of understanding of his audience wouldn't allow him to start with Jesus, he backed up and started at the beginning!"

Bible Reference:
1 Corinthians 1:23

"That is powerful," Greg agreed.

Bernard asked the final comparative question: "What did Paul do and say to challenge and correct their faulty worldview concepts?"

"He complimented them for seeking to know God in verse 22 where he says they were 'very religious.' Then Paul used what he had seen of their religion, the many idols, and the altar to the unknown God, as a platform from which to preach," responded Diana.

"Yes," added Miriam, "and he also quoted their poets as a door opener. I think that kept Paul relevant to his hearers. Because they realized he was well read and knew something about them, they were more inclined to listen."

Epicureans/Stoics

Where on the Scale?
-11 to -12

Understood which of the 8 gospel concepts?
None

Where did Paul begin to witness and why?
With Jesus and Cross, but dropped back to God and creation when he perceived their lack of understanding

Since the audiences had different understandings of biblical content, the evangelists started at different points in God's redemptive story and gave more information as was needed. We need to learn from these examples.

The group sat silently for a moment looking at their work on the three sheets before them. Each one realized the significance of this study. It had the potential to drastically transform their ministry.

Greg glanced at his watch and realized their time was almost up. Surely Amber had the kids in the rooms getting showered and dressed for supper by now. Soon they would enjoy Mexican cuisine and laugh together around the table as good friends do. Then they would turn in early and leave for Frankfurt in the morning. The retreat was nearly over. Now was the time for a decision. He was ready.

Greg looked at Diana and realized she was already studying him with a tenuous smile. Could she see on his face what was going on in his mind?

"Well, here goes, team," he began. "As significant as our work on the parables and the scale was …" Then he paused.

Diana's mind was going a mile a minute. *Oh no, he still wants to pack up and head back to America. Well, I'll just have to adjust. God has led me through my husband before, and He will again. I'll go wherever He leads us.*

Greg continued, "I mean, as much as we learned from Jesus' teaching in the parable of the soils and the need for tilling evangelism before we do planting and finally reaping evangelism …" Another pause.

He's really going to leave, thought Diana. She took a deep breath and prayed a quick prayer for help. *I don't want to cry. I want to be brave and support Greg in his decision.*

"Even though," started the next sentence.

Even though, she thought, *that's not good.*

"Even though," he continued, "we learned so much during the first two days of this retreat that could transform our ministry here."

Diana closed her eyes.

"This material on the gospel communication process, worldview noise, and the biblical examples of dealing with audiences of different worldviews has *really* opened my eyes. I can see now that no matter where we serve, we are going to have to deal with people's worldviews. We also will need to share the gospel in worldview-relevant ways. Thanks so much Bern and Miri, and Di, too, for helping me learn these important truths from God's Word."

Here it comes, Diana thought.

96

After a long pause Greg added, "Would you honor Diana and me by taking the lead in the church-planting team in Frankfurt"—a short pause—"and allowing us to serve by your side?"

Diana's eyes and mouth shot wide open! As Bernard responded affirmatively, she jumped up from her chair and crossed the room. Greg was up, too, and the two embraced as the tears began to flow. Diana had not wanted to cry, but these were tears of joy. Obviously, details needed to be worked out, but it was decided: the Tillmans were staying in Germany. They would continue to work with their friends, the Sämanns. They would continue to learn and apply Good Soil principles. Tonight's supper at the Mexican restaurant would be a true celebration.

How Can We Know What They Believe?
Peeling the Worldview Onion

Where does the time go? thought Greg. He had just finished his quiet time with God and was sitting at his computer reviewing his calendar. After their retreat in Kaiserslautern, they had been busy with the catch-up that is the result of being away. Also, ministry had kept them busy. Now he realized twelve weeks had flown by. It wasn't as if they hadn't talked. The couples had planning meetings and ministered together all throughout the three months. But with the day-to-day business, they had not talked more about the concepts they learned together on the retreat. Today he and Diana were going to meet Bern and Miri for most of the day to do more *Good Soil Strategizing* as they had come to call it.

It wasn't that they weren't applying their findings either. Each of the four believed they were improving their evangelism efforts by *slowing down* the process. *Slowing down* evangelism sounded strange, but it was what they were doing, and even if it was not speeding up church planting, it definitely was making it better. They were seeking to help their hearers truly understand the gospel and move up the scale by tilling the soil. They also saw many of their contacts moving across the scale as a result of deepening relationships that were opening hearts to hear the gospel.

An email Greg sent to Joe, his administrator, yesterday summed up well how he was feeling.

New Message	_ ↗ ✕
Recipients: joeshepherd@missions.org	
Subject: Greetings from Germany	

Joe,

Greetings from "spring-is-finally-on-its-way" Germany. Today we saw buds on the trees in the park. I'm excited about Easter ministry possibilities as we see warmer temperatures.

These weeks since the retreat have been great. Not only have we continued to learn so much from Bern and Miri, but we are seeing a difference in people's responses in evangelism and in the discipling of our little band. In our Sunday Bible study I had people look up verses with *suniemi*, *paradechomai*, and *katecho* in them to help solidify their concept of understand, embrace, and retain as it relates to the gospel in the parable of the soils. What fun it was! The interaction of the activity was fun, sure, but even more fun was the seeing lights come on as they understood. I'm attaching a copy (in English, of course) of the study we did if you're interested.

Thanks for your prayers. We thank God for His Word, for great colleagues, and for your encouragement along the way.

Yours and His for a harvest,

Greg

GoodSoilstudy.docx

Send

As Greg was about to shut down his computer and get ready to go to the meeting, it chimed and a little box popped up indicating he had a new message. It was Joe. Normally he wouldn't be receiving a message from Joe at this hour of the day since Germany is five hours ahead of North American (Eastern Standard) time. But Joe was on a trip visiting missionaries under his care in Western Europe. He was in Italy with Giuseppe and Carlita DeLuca and would arrive in Germany later this week. Greg looked at his watch and decided he had time to open the email and read it quickly if it was not too long.

Re: Greetings from Germany _ ⤢ ✕

From: joeshepherd@missions.org

Greg,

We are having a good time with the missionaries here in Italy. They are a great group. I have shared a bit about the *good soil* discoveries your team has been making. They are interested in hearing more—not only here in Italy, but in Spain, Portugal, and

England where I have already visited. I'd like to talk with you and Bern about making it our emphasis at our All-Western Europe Conference in November. It might be good for the two of you to run your colleagues through the learning processes you have experienced.

Eager to see you on Thursday,

Joe

📎 DeLucaFamily-Italy.jpg

[Send]

With a couple of clicks Greg was out of his server, the computer was shutting down, and he was on his way out the office door. "Honey," he shouted down the stairs as he took them two at a time, "you'll never guess what Joe wants us to do at the All-Europe this year."

Because the foursome was so eager to delve into their work again after three months, everyone was on time. They shared prayer requests, prayed, and started the meeting.

Bernard began. "It's been quite awhile since we worked on this together, but we have been applying the principles we learned, so it may not be quite as difficult to answer my question as it may first appear." With that he unrolled and posted their "Best Ideas" list on the wall and asked, "Does anyone have a *best idea* to add to our list either from our last meeting or from something that has come up these last weeks?"

"No problem there," Diana responded quickly. "I believe one of us said something like, 'the greater the difference between the gospel recipient's worldview and a biblical worldview, the more dense the worldview noise will be, hence, the greater possibility for not understanding.' I've seen that often. I see a huge difference in 'noise' between when I share with nominal Catholics and people from the Eastern community."

"Okay, good," encouraged Bernard, writing the statement on the paper. "Someone else?"

> *The greater the difference between the gospel recipient's worldview and a biblical worldview, the more dense the worldview noise will be, hence, the greater possibility for not understanding.*

"Yes," answered Miriam. "Do you remember when we were studying the passages of Peter and Paul preaching to different audiences? We learned that when the audiences knew less biblical content, the evangelists in the New Testament started earlier in God's redemptive story and gave more information as needed. I'm finding that if I do that with friends who have virtually no Bible knowledge, I see far better results than when I used to just try to 'share Christ.' Giving them some biblical context enables them to make a better, more educated response."

> *The crucial eternal life and death question we need to ask is "How much Bible content and biblical context does an unbeliever need in order to make a good soil faith response?"*

"Excellent!" exclaimed Bernard. "So the crucial eternal life and death question we need to ask is 'How much Bible *content* and biblical *context* does an unbeliever need in order to make a *good soil* faith response?' Right?"

"I think you're both right," Greg commented. "And that relates to a *best idea* I've been chewing on: When Paul realized the worldview and lack of understanding of his audience in Athens wouldn't allow him to start with Jesus, he backed up and started at the beginning. But we won't always have clear-cut indications such as we see in the New Testament. How do we determine what people know and/or believe about God and the Bible so we know where we need to start?"

Bernard finished writing Greg's observation on the paper, then swung back around, clicking the top on the marker. "That's such an important question, Greg. Thanks. And it's one that I was hoping we could work on today. You'll notice our *best ideas* today relate to worldviews since we worked on that last and, praise the Lord, we have been trying out these principles for the past three months." Bernard pulled out a large piece of card stock he had already prepared and showed it to the group. "Just so we are sure we are on the same page," he continued, "here is a simple definition of *worldview* we can use as we deal with these concepts." (See margin.)

Worldview:
a perspective through which an individual sees and interprets life

"Every rational human being possesses a worldview and behaves more or less consistently with that worldview. Each person's worldview includes foundational beliefs that must be aligned with the essential gospel truths taught in the Bible in order for him to possess genuine saving faith in Jesus Christ. When a person chooses to trust Jesus and places his faith in Jesus alone for salvation, he rejects his previous false beliefs. This core worldview change is repentance, a turning around 180 degrees. That's our goal. Now, do you remember how we defined 'worldview noise'?"

Our Best Ideas

1. The gospel is not only a truth; it is many truths.

2. What can I do with the time I have? That is all God wants me to do.

3. The time we spend on each piece of God's story depends on where the unbeliever is on the scale.

4. Our task is moving unbelievers up the scale from darkness to light.

5. Love, integrity, and time help move unbelievers "across" the scale from being closed to open to the gospel.

6. The scale is not to be understood as people having to move rigidly through each point or even in the same order.

7. The conversion of unbelievers can be a gradual process that leads to the instantaneous point of regeneration.

Best Ideas Cont'd

8. The greater the difference between the gospel recipient's worldview and a biblical worldview, the more dense the worldview noise will be and hence, the greater possibility for not understanding.

9. Since the target audiences had different understandings of biblical content, the evangelists in the New Testament started at different points in God's redemptive story and gave more information as was needed.

10. When Paul realized that the worldview and lack of understanding of his audience wouldn't allow him to start with Jesus, he backed up and started at the beginning.

Diana let out a burst of air. "Well," she started slowly, but picked up speed as she realized she remembered. "Worldview noise is the effect of the unbiblical elements in an unbeliever's worldview belief system that *confuse* his understanding of essential gospel truths and/or that *predispose* him to reject the gospel."

"Very good! And that is why early on in the evangelism process it is important to know what the person to whom we are witnessing believes about the core issues of life," Bernard explained. Then, to everyone's surprise he pulled out two onions, a knife, and a cutting board. He cleared a space on the coffee table in front of him, placed the cutting board on the table and the onion on the board, then *whack*, he sliced through one of the onions.

Worldview noise: the effect of the unbiblical elements in one's worldview belief system that confuse his understanding of gospel truths and/ or predispose him to reject the gospel.

"Whoa, easy there, big guy!" Miriam cautioned.

"What?" he asked, laughing. "Don't you like my visuals?" Then he turned their focus to his illustration. "Let's say this onion represents each one of us and our belief systems. The onion has a core and we have core beliefs. The onion has several layers that protect the core; people have layers that we must get through if we would understand a person's core beliefs. In peeling onions, there are three ways to get to the core. One is like I just did—stab straight into the onion and cut out the core. It may be effective if we want to season hamburger with it, but if we try to do that with people, we'll either leave them bleeding by the side of the road or we'll shut them down. They won't want to talk to us."

"Been there, done that," sighed Greg. "There's got to be a better way."

"The second way to peel an onion is to do nothing but scratch around endlessly on the surface. We might get a couple of the thin paperlike layers off, but we're not going to get to the real meat of the onion. In the same way, just scratching the surface with people, we'll not truly understand their world-

view. *Liebling*," Bernard addressed Miriam, "would you peel this other onion the way you do to make your famous onion rings?"

Miriam took the onion and deftly peeled away, beginning by taking off all the outside, unusable layers. She then scored the next two layers and carefully peeled them away in halves, then cut the halves into quarters. She repeated this process several times to get quarter moon shapes.

Meanwhile Bernard explained: "These aren't normal onion rings; in fact, they aren't even rings at all. But they are a delicious treat Miri has been making for years. She learned it from her mother. The quarter moon shapes she ends up with are battered and fried like traditional onion rings. But what we have when we are done are edible 'spoons' which are ideal for scooping up salsa and popping the whole thing into your mouth."

"I remember having these at your place last year," Greg commented, salivating. "Are we going to have them today?"

"Why not?" answered Miri. "I've already got some cut!"

"Yes, I'm always ready to have Miri's onion rings," added Bernard, "but the point is this: to get to the core of the onion using all of the layers for 'scoop spoons,' Miri peels layer by layer. There may be a quicker way, but that is how she goes about it for this recipe. And *that* is how we need to peel worldview onions: carefully one layer at a time.

"… that is how we need to peel worldview onions: carefully one layer at a time."

"Diana, you're the artist. Can you draw an onion like this one I've cut through the middle?" As Diana drew on the flip chart, Bernard continued talking, using his cut onion to illustrate. Pointing to the core, he said, "The core of the onion represents a person's core beliefs. These are at the center of his worldview, and everything he does is influenced by them. A person's core beliefs are initially influenced by his culture and/or subculture. They change only through crisis or confrontation."

Diana was done with the drawing so Bernard thanked her, drew an arrow pointing to the core, and called the arrow *Core Beliefs*.

1. Core Beliefs

"Now," continued Bernard, "if everything a person does is influenced by his core beliefs, what does that really mean? How would we label some of these other layers we have to get through to learn a person's core beliefs?"

Greg let out a whistle. "Well, I guess we're dealing with choices, values, conduct, maybe habits, the way someone does things regularly—how am I doing? Are there more?"

"That's great," Bernard responded. "Those are the same types of things I was thinking. I figure that a person's core beliefs shape his values," and with that Bernard began to write. "That would be the layer next to the core. Values grow out of core beliefs, and personal choices then are cultivated from our values. As we make choices consistent with our worldview, over time, we develop behavioral patterns." Bernard stopped drawing arrows and turned to the group.

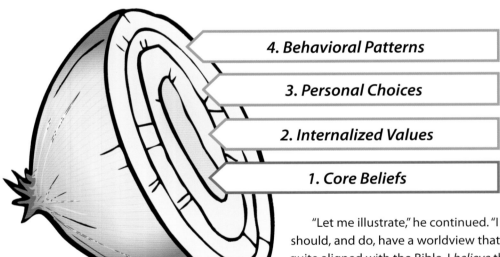

4. *Behavioral Patterns*

3. *Personal Choices*

2. *Internalized Values*

1. *Core Beliefs*

"Let me illustrate," he continued. "I should, and do, have a worldview that is quite aligned with the Bible. I *believe* that the God of the Bible created the universe and all that is in it, including me," Bernard said as he pointed to *Core Beliefs*. "As His creation and His child, I desire to worship Him; worshipping God is an important *value* to me." With this he pointed to point number two. "Because worshipping God with His people is so important to me, I *choose* to go to church—it's one of my personal choices. In fact, this has become a *pattern* with me. I go every week and thus my behavioral pattern has become observable. You see how my core beliefs about God and

the world shape my life all the way out to my behavioral patterns. Now, can someone give us another example?"

"Sure!" Diana spoke up, standing and pointing to the layers as she spoke. "A typical secular, materialistic person doesn't believe in God, but instead figures that this life is all there is. He *believes* in the quote from the Bible oddly enough—1 Corinthians 15:32—'Let us eat and drink, for tomorrow we die.' So, on Sunday he *values* his rest and sleeps in, not going to church. He *chooses* to go out on his boat all afternoon and party all night. He does this quite regularly to the extent that it is a *pattern* for him to wake up hung over, feel terrible on Monday, and struggle to get through the day."

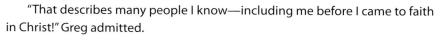

Bible Reference:
1 Corinthians 15:32

"That describes many people I know—including me before I came to faith in Christ!" Greg admitted.

"I know what you mean," Bernard assured him. "But look at how the onion helps us understand where people are coming from just by observing their lives. It will work for all worldviews. And we can do more than just observe; we can ask questions. That is what peeling the onion is all about. You see, we can call the outside, or the surface of the onion, *human commonalities*. We have much of life in common with other people: we work, we have health issues, we travel, we have hobbies, etc. So as we meet someone for the first time, we start there, with human commonalities. We don't cut right to the core. Remember, that could hurt! *Entry Conversations* would be a good label for this stage. As we get to know someone, we carefully peel layer by layer, asking *Investigative Questions*. Only then, as we get a grasp on a person's worldview, do we start *Conversion Discussions* that can bring that person to the point of changing his worldview, repenting, and putting his trust in Christ."

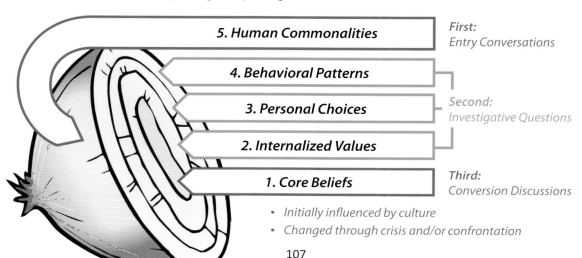

5. Human Commonalities — *First: Entry Conversations*

4. Behavioral Patterns

3. Personal Choices — *Second: Investigative Questions*

2. Internalized Values

1. Core Beliefs — *Third: Conversion Discussions*

- *Initially influenced by culture*
- *Changed through crisis and/or confrontation*

"Now remember, what we are trying to do in 'peeling the worldview onion' is discover where a person is on the scale so we can determine where to begin in sharing the gospel. We *don't* want to attack a person's worldview offensively or cause an unnecessary argument," Bernard warned. "The gospel itself, when we share it, will do its own offending."[8]

> **"Our goal should be to initiate conversations with people that may become redemptive relationships."**

"Our goal should be to initiate conversations with people that may become redemptive relationships," observed Miriam. "We peel back layers, getting to know them and what they value. But our overall objective is to share the gospel in a form that is relevant to their worldview."

"Oh, I like that!" exclaimed Diana. "That should be one of our *best ideas*: Initiate conversations that may become redemptive relationships."

Bible Reference:
Colossians 4:2-6

"Okay, we'll get that on the list. And she's right, the onion-peeling guides us in sharing the gospel," Bernard added. "Paul asked the Colossians to pray for him that 'God may open to us a door for the word, to declare the mystery of Christ' and that he would *make it clear, which is how I ought to speak* (Colossians 4:2-6). He also wanted *their* speech to always 'be gracious, seasoned with salt, so that you may know how you ought to answer each person.' Peeling the onion will help us with that."

"Wow, this is powerful," commented Greg. "Could we just brainstorm a bit on each part of the peeling? For example, what do we want to say and ask at each level?"

The group had been up and down, throwing out ideas, writing, jousting verbally. Finally they all sat down, let out a collective sigh, and looked at their work.

Miriam broke the silence. "I think we have something here. You know, my psych and counseling professors were always saying things like 'most people in the world are lonely' and 'most people like to talk about themselves.' This approach is something we should be able to use without much difficulty, and it will help us tremendously as we seek to share the good news about Jesus with others."

---

8 Paul advised the Corinthians to "Give no offense to Jews or to Greeks or to the church of God" (1 Corinthians 10:32) in "whatever you do" (v. 31). But earlier in the book he was clear that when we "preach Christ crucified," it would be "a stumbling block to Jews and folly to Gentiles" (1:23). Peter also said that for "those who do not believe," Jesus is a "stone of stumbling and a rock of offense" (1 Peter 2:7-8 quoting Isaiah 8:14).

First: Entry Conversations

Look for "entry points" in order to get deeper into worldview layers

- Issues involving personal pain or crisis
- Sources of enjoyment or personal significance
- Religious expressions or symbols
- Overt statements of beliefs, values, and value-driven choices
- Observed behavioral patterns that reflect values and beliefs

◄ *The group brainstormed for several minutes and came up with the following list of descriptors and examples for each level of onion-peeling.*

Second: Investigative Questions

Probe politely to discover core beliefs

- As trust is built address deeper issues
- Do not be judgmental or argumentative
- Examples: "Ever think about how the world got here?"
  "If asked, 'What happens when people die?' what would you say?"

Third: Conversion Discussions

The conversion of core beliefs generally occurs during the presentation of the gospel, as the weaknesses in an unbeliever's worldview are exposed to the appealing truths of God's Word.

- A crisis can crack the core
- Avoid jumping into gospel presentation before fully peeling the onion
- Even though peeling is not our final goal, it still must not be rushed

Exercise #11:

Do you have any other examples to add to this list?

"Anybody can do this," assured Diana.

"And everybody—every Christian—should," added Bern.

The foursome sat silently for a while longer allowing the importance and potential of their discoveries to sink in more. Then suddenly Greg blurted out, "That reminds me," slapping his hand to his head. "Joe Shepherd wrote today. He wants us to share what we've been learning with our colleagues at the All-Western Europe Conference next November."

"What?" asked Bernard. "What will that involve?"

"I don't know for sure," answered Greg. "But I do know we're talking about training a couple hundred people. Joe's coming to Frankfurt on Thursday and wants to talk with us about it."

This time it was Bernard who let out a low whistle. "Well, I guess we'll worry about that when we find out more on Thursday. It sounds like a daunting challenge, but also a great opportunity to influence others positively for the cause of evangelism and discipleship. For now, let's take some *best ideas* and pray that God will help us to peel worldview onions well so our evangelistic efforts can be more effective."

Our Best Ideas

1. The gospel is not only a truth; it is many truths.

2. What can I do with the time I have? That is all God wants me to do.

3. The time we spend on each piece of God's story depends on where the unbeliever is on the scale.

4. Our task is moving unbelievers up the scale from darkness to light.

5. Love, integrity, and time help move unbelievers "across" the scale from being closed to open to the gospel.

6. The scale is not to be understood as people having to move rigidly through each point or even in the same order.

7. The conversion of unbelievers can be a gradual process that leads to the instantaneous point of regeneration.

Best Ideas (cont'd)

8. The greater the difference between the gospel recipient's worldview and a biblical worldview, the more dense the worldview noise will be and hence, the greater possibility for not understanding.

9. Since the target audiences had different understandings of biblical content, the evangelists in the New Testament started at different points in God's redemptive story and gave more information as was needed.

10. When Paul realized that the worldview and lack of understanding of his audience wouldn't allow him to start with Jesus, he backed up and started at the beginning, with God.

Best Ideas (cont'd)

11. How much Bible content and biblical context does an unbeliever need in order to make a Good Soil decision?

12. Initiate conversations that may become redemptive relationships.

13. Our overall objective is to share the gospel in a form that is relevant to our hearer's worldview.

Exercise #12:

By the end of their study, the group came up with 13 "Best Ideas" to remember. Which ones do you think apply most to you and your ministry?

What Do They Need to Know? (Part 1)

How Much Bible Content and Biblical Context Does Each Unbeliever Need in Order to Make a "Good Soil" Faith Response?

"Try to relax, Bern," Greg encouraged.

The two families and Amber were 32,000 feet in the air somewhere between Frankfurt, Germany, and Lisbon, Portugal, on their way to the All-Western Europe Conference, but it wasn't the flight that was making Bernard nervous.

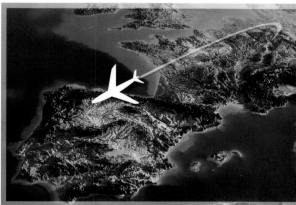

Greg continued, "We have the whole seminar organized; we've gone over the material several times, and we've confirmed our methodology. We'll be fine."

"I suppose you're right," Bernard replied. "It's just that there will be so many workers there with plenty of years of experience. Who are we to teach them anything?"

Available from: 🔖
www.GoodSoil.com

"Nobodies!" Greg was quick to respond with a laugh. "And we *shouldn't* be teaching if we had any other attitude but yours. We *are* nobodies except for the grace of God in our lives, that's for *sure*. But that's just it; He *has been* working. If over a year ago we tried to get up in front of people and teach them, it would have been the blind leading the blind. But we've learned so much and practiced what we learned, so we can go to this conference and teach with confidence. That chronological Bible study book you developed with Diana's artwork …"

Bernard interrupted, "What do you mean? You worked on it, too!"

"Please!" Greg responded. "I read through it, looking for errors. It is mostly your work. But as I was saying, that book has been tremendous in helping people understand the gospel."

"But the ChronoBridge in the back of the book was a joint effort going back to our original retreat," Bernard continued to protest. "And the bridge has helped greatly in bringing people to the point of embracing the gospel."

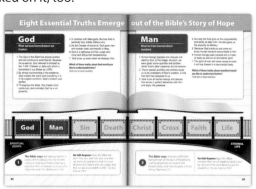

"That's true," Greg admitted. "So before we develop into a full-blown mutual admiration society, can we just agree that God has taught us some things that could be valuable to other people and trust Him to use us in this conference?"

Bernard took in a deep breath and let it out with a sigh. "Okay. But I want you to know I am grateful to be part of a team with you and Diana and that we're doing this together."

"Likewise, buddy. Likewise."

After arriving in Lisbon, the group grabbed their bags and joined approximately one hundred colleagues, loading two busses going to the Algarve, Portugal's southern coast. Within minutes they were outside the city and speeding over the seventeen-kilometer-long Vasco de Gama Bridge crossing the Tejo River. The two-and-one-half-hour ride took them over the beautiful rolling hills of the Alentejo farming region until they climbed the southern chain of mountains and dropped down to sea level once again. Once at the coast, they turned west to the town of Albufeira where the conference facility was located.

The other one hundred leaders flew into Faro, the leading city of the southern coast of Portugal, and were shuttled in vans the remaining forty-five kilometers to Albufeira. Missionaries from Greg and Diana's mission and the international pastors and partners working with them came from Belgium, England, France, Germany, Ireland, Italy, Luxembourg, Portugal, and Spain.

The two hundred-meter-square conference room was set up with thirty round tables to accommodate the two hundred attendees. According to plan, the German team led their student-colleagues through interactive methods using very little lecture. In this way, the missionaries and pastors made the material their own as they "discovered" the truths for themselves.

On the first day Bernard, Miriam, Greg, and Diana started with the Parable of the Soils (Chapter 1 of this

114

book) to teach the importance of helping unbelievers understand, embrace, and retain the gospel. Then they talked about the Good Soil Evangelism and Discipleship Scale (Chapter 2) and taught about initial contact and relational evangelism (Chapters 4 and 5). Next the foursome walked their colleagues through the gospel communication process (Chapter 6).

During the second day they worked through the worldview case studies in Acts (Chapter 7) and introduced "peeling onions" (Chapter 8).

By the end of the second day virtually everyone was on board with the Good Soil approach to church planting: slowing down evangelism to speed up church planting. Missionaries from nearly all the countries realized the need for a different approach but weren't sure what it might be. All the teams were already doing well in developing friendships, having understood the need in the postmodern world for an emphasis on relational evangelism. During a break, Greg and Bernard discovered that missionaries in Portugal and Spain had already been using interactive chronological Bible studies similar to the one they had developed, so they asked representatives from those countries to share their experiences the next day.

> *By the end of the second day virtually everyone was on board with the Good Soil approach to church planting: slowing down evangelism to speed up church planting.*

After the worship time that opened the third day, Greg addressed the crowd, "Without looking back at your notes, take two minutes as table groups to determine: 'What is our major task as we deal with people located on the bottom half of the Good Soil E&D Scale?' Once you decide, try to come up with the three levels of that task." He set the alarm on his watch and said, "Go!"

Two minutes later, Bernard shouted, "Stop!" As the class quieted down, he asked, "Okay, what is our task at the bottom half of the scale?"

Almost in unison the group said, "Evangelism."

Impressed with the strong response, Bernard exclaimed, "Wow! Very good. Now, the table in the back in the middle; yes, you folks, give us one of the levels of evangelism."

The leader of the table group replied, "Tilling evangelism."

"Good," Bernard complimented. "How about over here," he said, pointing to his left at a table of all women, "What is the next level?"

A redhead with a broad smile responded, "Planting evangelism."

"That's right. And the final level of evangelism? The far right front table."

Counts cost of a faith response	**-1**	**Level 3:**
Confronted with a faith response	**-2**	*Reaping Evangelism*
Senses personal spiritual conviction	**-3**	7. Persuade
Understands some gospel concepts*	**-4**	6. Personalize 5. Clarity
Interested in Jesus and the gospel	**-5**	**Level 2:**
Exposed to other Christian concepts	**-6**	*Planting Evangelism*
Realizes there is only one true God	**-7**	4. Establish uniqueness of Jesus 3. Teach gospel concepts
Vulnerable to false religious beliefs	**-8**	**Level 1:**
Seeks to fill personal spiritual void	**-9**	*Tilling Evangelism*
Senses personal spiritual emptiness	**-10**	2. Challenge core worldview
Aware of higher Power or powers	**-11**	1. Model, love, & pray
Born with a God-Vacuum	**-12**	

Mark 4:20 / *Matthew 13:23*

From that table a dark-haired, strong-jawed man in his thirties answered in a strong Castilian accent, "Reaping evangelism."

Both Bernard and Greg were on their feet, tag-teaming so nicely that the audience didn't know who would speak next. This time it was Greg. "Excellent. Now we'd like you to think of that bottom half of the scale and those three levels of evangelism. Let's start up at level 3, reaping evangelism. Here is the question."

Bernard finished the phrase. "What gospel-related knowledge do people *not* possess at each of these three major stages? First, think of people who are at the -4 level on the Good Soil Scale. What do people not know about the gospel at the -4 level? You'll have four minutes to brainstorm. Begin!"

When four minutes had passed, Greg quieted the crowd, and said, "Okay. Let's have popcorn responses—one from each table—in no particular order. Just have your leader stand and shout out one gospel-related bit of knowledge that an unbeliever does not know at the -4 level. Who will be first?"

From all over the room, in all kinds of accents, came the answers.

"Jesus is not 'one way' but the 'only way' to God."

An American shouted, "Jesus is not 'one way' but the 'only way' to God."

116

"My sins will be forgiven if I trust Jesus alone as Savior," was the contribution from a youth worker in Luxembourg.

"Jesus died in my place to pay the penalty for my sins," added a pastor from Belgium.

"Jesus arose from the dead—God has power over death!" and "None of my 'good deeds' gain me favor before God," came from a young American couple.

Then a Portuguese pastor's wife affirmed, "I must choose to receive or to reject God's provision."

When the "popcorn" slowed a bit, Bernard challenged the group, "Okay, now think about the planting level, concentrating on -7. What do unbelievers not understand about the gospel when they are down at -7 on the Good Soil Scale?"

Again the responses were as varied as the nationalities of the people who shared.

"Disobedience to God offends Him greatly—it is 'sin.'"

"We went back a bit further at our table. The Bible is God's Word to mankind."

Bernard responded to that comment, "Good. Somewhere along a person's journey to faith the Bible has to be established as authoritative, as from God. Let's hear some more."

"After death, I will face God in judgment for my sins."

"God has a plan to provide for the forgiveness of my sins."

"Jesus Christ is God's Son."

"Jesus was innocent, but evil people crucified Him."

As the answers slowed, Greg stated, "Very good. Did you notice how the deficiencies in gospel knowledge at level -4 and up had more to do with Jesus and our response to Him, while at -7 through -5 we didn't see that as much. We will see an even bigger difference as we drop down to -11 on the scale. In your groups think through the deficiencies in gospel knowledge a person has who is at -11. You will have four more minutes. Begin."

Deficiencies: what unbelievers do NOT know

The four minutes passed quickly and once again short answers were shared. Three different Americans were first: "The highest power is God—there is only one true living God."

"Yes, and that God is the Creator of the world and all that is in it."

"This God is eternal, personal, holy, just, and loving."

Then a tiny Italian lady with a big voice bellowed, "Alienation from this God has caused my emptiness." And from the same table her colleague added, "There are no human efforts that will fill this void."

"But there is hope for me that I can possess, here and now," clarified another.

"What and in whom I believe does matter—eternally," a college student from Ireland commented.

Finally, a French pastor in the back of the room contributed, "There is life after death, and I must prepare for it."

Miriam and Diana had been taking turns writing down the responses as they were shared. Bernard waited for Diana to finish writing, then stood.

Referring to the flip charts, he said, "Can you see how at different levels there are different gospel knowledge deficiencies? People either know very little, some, or a good deal about the gospel. As we 'peel their onions' we begin to see what they do and don't understand about the gospel. Based on their knowledge, here is the crucial eternal life and death question: **How much *Bible content* and *biblical context* does each unbeliever need in order to make a *good soil* faith response?** That is the question we need to ask

Here are the group's completed Gospel Knowledge Deficiencies Charts after a team put them in logical order. ➥

Counts cost of a faith response	-1
Confronted with a faith response	-2
Senses personal spiritual conviction	-3
Understands some gospel concepts	-4

Level 3:

Reaping Evangelism

←

Gospel Knowledge Deficiencies for Level -4
- Once I trust Jesus as my Savior I will never regret it.
- I must choose to receive or to reject God's provision.
- The new "tug in my heart" is God drawing me to Himself.
- My sins will be forgiven if I trust Jesus alone as Savior.
- None of my "good deeds" bring me into favor with God.
- Jesus arose from the dead—God has power over death!
- Jesus died in my place, to pay the penalty for my sins.
- Jesus is not "one way" but the "only way" to God.

ourselves as we get to know people and their worldviews. In other words, where do we begin? How much do we need to share with them so they truly understand? Let's take a fifteen-minute break. When we come back we will see how Jesus might have responded to these questions."

Interested in Jesus and the gospel	-5
Exposed to other Christian concepts	-6
Realizes there is only one true God	-7

Level 2:
Planting Evangelism

←

Gospel Knowledge Deficiencies for Level -7
- Jesus was innocent but evil people crucified Him.
- Jesus Christ is God's special Son.
- God has a plan to provide for the forgiveness of my sins.
- After death, I will face God in judgment for my sins.
- Disobedience to God offends Him greatly—it is "sin."
- The Bible is God's Word to mankind.

Vulnerable to false religious beliefs	-8
Seeks to fill personal spiritual void	-9
Senses personal spiritual emptiness	-10
Aware of higher Power or powers	-11
Born with a God-Vacuum	-12

Level 1:
Tilling Evangelism

←

Gospel Knowledge Deficiencies for Level -11
- What and whom I believe does matter—eternally.
- There is life after death and I must prepare for it.
- There is hope for me that I can possess, here and now.
- There are no human efforts that will fill this void.
- Alienation from this God has caused my emptiness.
- This God is the Creator of the world and all that is in it.
- This God is eternal, personal, holy, just, and loving.
- The highest power is God—only one true living God.

What Do They Need to Know? (Part 2)
Jesus' Answer and the Essential Gospel Concepts

The group was reassembling and settling down, eager to get back to the study. Bernard stated the same question asked before break: **"How much *Bible content* and *biblical context* does each unbeliever need in order to make a *good soil* faith response?** Let's listen to Jesus' response to that question. Open your Bibles to Luke 24:13-27. Please read the verses with a view to answering this question: 'To explain God's redemptive plan, where did Jesus begin?' Have a volunteer at your table read the passage out loud while everyone else follows along. When you are done, have everyone at your table stand and stretch."

Bible Reference:
Luke 24:13-27

That very day two of them were going to a village named Emmaus, about seven miles from Jerusalem, and they were talking with each other about all these things that had happened. While they were talking and discussing together, Jesus himself drew near and went with them. But their eyes were kept from recognizing him.

And he said to them, "What is this conversation that you are holding with each other as you walk?" And they stood still, looking sad. Then one of them, named Cleopas, answered him, "Are you the only visitor to Jerusalem who does not know the things that have happened there in these days?" And he said to them, "What things?"

And they said to him, "Concerning Jesus of Nazareth, a man who was a prophet mighty in deed and word before God and all the people, and how our chief priests and rulers delivered him up to be condemned to death, and crucified him. But we had hoped that he was the one to redeem Israel. Yes, and besides all this, it is now the third day since these things happened. Moreover, some women of our company amazed us. They were at the tomb early in the morning, and when they did not find his body, they came back saying that they had even seen a vision of angels, who said that he was alive. Some of those who were with us went to the tomb and found it just as the women had said, but him they did not see."

> **Exercise #13:**
>
> *As you read, highlight text that helps you answer the question, "To explain God's redemptive plan, where did Jesus begin?"*

And he said to them, "O foolish ones, and slow of heart to believe all that the prophets have spoken! Was it not necessary that the Christ should suffer these things and enter into his glory?" And beginning with Moses and all the Prophets, he interpreted to them in all the Scriptures the things concerning himself.

After everyone was standing, Greg said, "You may be seated again. Thank you. Now what does 'beginning with Moses and all the prophets' mean?"

A lanky Englishman lifted his voice and responded, "The Jews had a few different ways to refer to the Scriptures. For example, they divided them into three parts: the Law, which would be the first five books; the Writings, the Psalms and other poetry; and the Prophets. But sometimes they would refer simply to the Law and the Prophets. 'Moses' most likely refers to the first five books, which he wrote, and 'the prophets' refers to the major and minor prophets. This may very well have been a way for Jesus to refer to the whole Old Testament."

"Excellent. So on at least this one occasion, Jesus apparently thought a good grasp of the Old Testament was essential to truly understand His life, death, and resurrection. The events of the Old Testament gave His disciples a foundation to perceive what happened in the New."

Bernard was up now. "This is a crucial truth. These were disciples of Jesus who did not 'get it' until He used the Old Testament to explain why He came. How can we expect postmoderns, centuries removed from Bible times, to understand if His disciples didn't? Consider our crucial eternal life and death question: How much Bible content and context do we need to share for a *good soil* faith response? when you respond to this next question."

Greg clicked the remote and read the question in big red letters on the screen. "How often have we shared from the *Old Testament* when giving a 'gospel presentation'?" He paused for effect, then said, "Jesus used it. Oh yeah, that's all He had!" Chuckles scattered throughout the room. "But seriously, Jesus told Old Testament stories and used Old Testament prophecies to help people *under-stand* the gospel. Maybe we should, too."

"Let's do one more exercise before Joe Shepherd, the executive administrator of our mission, comes to finish out the morning. Here it is: Make a list of the events *you think* Jesus may have used to explain Himself to His

Jesus told Old Testament stories and used Old Testament prophecies to help people understand the gospel. Maybe we should, too.

disciples. The trip to Emmaus would have taken two to three hours. Let's just say it took two. What Old Testament stories and prophecies do you think Jesus would have shared with them if He had two hours? Begin."

Exercise #14:

Before reading on, please do the same exercise, writing down what you think Jesus would have shared from the Old Testament.

Once again Bernard and Greg asked representatives from each table to share their findings while Miriam and Diana wrote the answers on flip charts on either side of the room. Below on the left are some of the stories the conference-goers shared. Some of the prophecies they thought Jesus would have used are on the right.

Old Testament Stories

Promise of the Satan Conqueror

Abraham and Isaac

The Passover
(and sacrificial lambs)

The Tabernacle

The Feasts of Israel
(telling the redemptive story of the Messiah)

Old Testament Prophecies

Psalm 2

Psalms 115-118

Isaiah 7:14

Isaiah 53

Micah 5:2

After the groups shared their work, Bernard addressed the crowd once more. "As we have given examples about people trusting Christ in our ministry in Germany, you've heard us talk about the evangelism tool we put together with twenty stories from the Old Testament and twenty from the New. This is why. From the Parable of the Soils we learned that *good soil* people *understand* the gospel. We believe that to understand the gospel our friends have to know about the God of the Bible and His plan for man. Jesus used the Old Testament to explain His person and work. We believe we need to use it, too. We'll talk more about this tool called *The Story of Hope* later, but for now, Joe is going to wrap up this session."

Joe came to the podium, and looking at the *Good Soil* group, said, "Thanks, Team Frankfurt, for sharing with us what you've learned as you've tried to reach your culture for Christ. These are great insights that should help us all in Western Europe and many other parts of the world."

Then, looking out across the room, he added, "Don't you think so?" The singular response was an outbreak of applause. Joe let the audience continue for a moment and then went on.

"What this team has been sharing with us fits in well with what D. A. Carson teaches and writes about. How many of you attended last year's Missionary Growth Conference and heard him speak?" About 20 percent of the group raised a hand. "Here is what Carson says.

> *The Bible as a whole document tells a story, and properly used, that story can serve … to shape our grasp of the entire Christian faith. In my view it is increasingly important to spell this out to Christians and to non-Christians alike—to Christians, to ground them in Scripture, and to non-Christians, as part of our proclamation of the gospel.*[9]

He believes that to share the gospel in a postmodern or pluralistic culture we must tell them the story of the Bible."

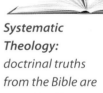

Systematic Theology: doctrinal truths from the Bible are organized into topical categories

Joe flipped to a blank slide and continued, "Modern man was scientific. If he could measure it or prove something scientifically, then it was true. As Carson says, our answer to modern man was systematic theology and clear-cut propositional evangelistic presentations." As he talked, boxes appeared one by one on the screen in an orderly fashion until the audience saw the completed slide at the bottom of the page.

"Besides that, modern man, for the most part, knew the Bible generally and considered it to be true. But, that is not the case anymore. The postmodern

Systematic Theology				
God	Scriptures	Angels	Mankind	Sin
Christ	Salvation	Holy Spirit	Church	Last Things

man says, 'There is no absolute truth, so how can anything be proven?' 'What works for me is good, what works for you is good. But don't try to convince me to change, because my way—whatever that way is—is just as good as yours.' Biblical theology approaches the Bible from a different perspective

---

9 D. A. Carson, *The Gagging of God* (Grand Rapids: Zondervan, 1996), 194.

Biblical Theology: seeks to understand theological truths as they are revealed progressively throughout the Bible

than systematic theology. Instead of dealing with a single topic using various passages to do so, biblical theology seeks to understand the redemptive story of God as it is revealed progressively, starting in the Old Testament and continuing through the New. Each text is dealt with in its historical context, building on the foundation of what came before."

Joe asked the group, "Now what or whom do we learn about first in the Bible? What is the first 'theology' so to speak?"

"We learn about God," the little Italian woman responded.

"Theology Proper," someone else shouted at the same time.

"In the beginning, God!" another added.

"That's right. Very good," Joe complimented the three participants as he clicked the remote. (See below for what appeared on the screen.) "And from Genesis 1:1 on, we learn more and more about God right through to Revelation 22.

God

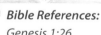

Bible References: Genesis 1:26

"Now what is the next major area of theology we learn?" Joe asked.

This time the tall Englishman was first to respond. "Anthropology."

"Good," Joe replied. "Genesis 1:26 says: 'Then God said, "Let us make man in our image, after our likeness. And let them have dominion over the fish of the sea and over the birds of the heavens and over the livestock and over all the earth and over every creeping thing that creeps on the earth.' Man was created by God to have a relationship with Him. He was created innocent but responsible to God with tasks to fulfill and commands to obey. And from there to the end of the Bible we learn more and more about man."

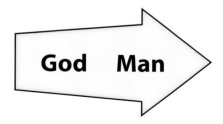

God   Man

Anticipating Joe's next question, a fiesty French woman in the back yelled, "*Zen mahn seened!*"

"Okay, thank you," Joe responded, chuckling. "'Then man sinned.' Sin is the next major doctrine we learn about chronologically, isn't it? And again, after we first learn of sin, we learn more and more as we continue to read the Bible. In fact, right away we learn that sin brings death." Joe clicked the remote two times. (See result below.) "In fact, as we read, we learn that physical, spiritual, and eternal death are all the result of sin. Our growing graph illustrates two things. The forward arrow symbolizes the time factor of progressive revelation—we learn as time goes on. The increasing width depicts the growing body of knowledge learned about each subject over time.

Zen mahn seened:
Then man sinned

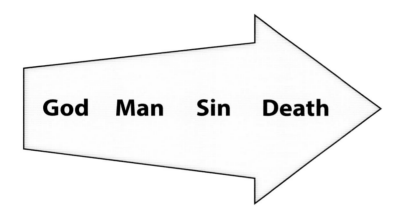

God   Man   Sin   Death

"This process continues throughout the Bible. As a new subject is introduced, we learn about it, but we do not cease to learn more about the previous subjects. All this happens as we read stories or narratives that are all woven into one big story or metanarrative."

A man on the left side of the room raised his hand.

"Yes?" Joe acknowledged the missionary.

"Uh, I, uh," he started slowly, then cleared his throat. "I really like what I've been learning at this conference. It sounds right and all. God knows we could be more effective in evangelism where we live. But those words up there on the screen look like a lot of other canned gospel outlines. It's just that, well, this one has eight points instead of four or five. Isn't this just another—what did Carson call it—Propositional presentation?"

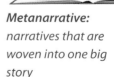

Metanarrative:
narratives that are
woven into one big
story

God Man Sin Death Christ Cross Faith Life

"Good catch. To tell you the truth, what you're looking at on this slide *is* the propositional gospel presentation Greg and Bern have included in the back of their evangelism resource *The Story of Hope*. I simply wanted to start this presentation using those eight words because I think it relates well to our biblical theology topic in two ways: it starts out with God (Theology Proper) and it is chronological in nature.

"Does that make sense? Even though it is a propositional presentation of the gospel, it is also chronological. We are looking at these essential gospel elements in the order in which they are revealed to humankind in the Bible. But let's get back to our comparison of systematic theology to biblical theology. They are both good ways to study the Bible but biblical theology may be better in sharing God's word with postmodern and pluralistic societies.

From the floor came the question, "What is biblical theology anyway? Are you saying that systematic theology is not biblical?"

"Good question." Joe replied. "We're not saying that at all. Both systematic theology and biblical theology are truly based on what we can learn from God's word, but, as one source says, the overall task of Biblical theology 'is to discern the coherence of the whole Bible as it unfolds over time. The key component … is the conviction that the Bible constitutes a single unified narrative.'[10] Biblical Theology focuses on the historical context of each text (especially taking into account what came before the text) while systematic theology looks at individual topics everywhere they are found in the Bible. Systematic theology follows themes; biblical theology follows the redemptive narrative flow."

---

10 Edward W. Klink III and Darian R. Lockett, *Understanding Biblical Theology*, p. 60.

With that, Joe changed the slide to reveal a rainbowlike image spreading across the screen. Then he continued, "As we already agreed, the Bible starts by revealing something— not a lot—about God. As we continue to read the story we learn more and more about Him, thus building our theology of God."

Joe clicked the remote and the word *God* slid across the screen and stopped at the top of the image in the blue stripe of the rainbow. Joe continued, "This illustrates how biblical theology traces the progressive revelation of God through history.

"But before we get to any mention of humankind in the Genesis account—remember our propositional gospel presentation went from God to Man—we actually see mentioned something about a person we know so much about today. But as we begin to read through the Old Testament we see very little of the Holy Spirit. The second verse of the Bible says that the 'Spirit of God was hovering over the face of the waters.' But then we don't see anything in Genesis about the Spirit of God until chapter six where God says His 'Spirit will not abide in man forever,' and we don't see anything about the Spirit again until Genesis 41:38 where Pharaoh asks his servants if they can find one 'in whom is the Spirit of God.' The Old Testament continues to be sparse on this topic." Joe clicked the remote and *Holy Spirit* flew across the screen and landed in the purple stripe of the rainbow.

Biblical Theology

Genesis 1:1

God
Holy Spirit
Mankind
Scriptures
Angels
Sin
Jesus Christ
Salvation
Last Things
Church

Revelation 22:21

Bible References:
Genesis 1:2
Genesis 6:3
Genesis 41:38

Joe continued, "So as we read through the Bible we progressively learn about mankind, the Scriptures, angels, etc." (Remote clicks accompanied each of these subjects until "etc." and then he filled out the illustration you can see above.) "God progressively revealed truths to mankind and we can study them in a manner consistent with the way He revealed them—looking for the first occurrences of doctrinal truths and then learning more about them as God gradually unveiled them to us in the progressing development of the Bible's Big Story. So, with Carson, I would suggest 'that a world both Biblically illiterate and sold out to philosophical pluralism demands that our proclamation of the gospel be a subset of Biblical theology.' [11]

"For now, I want to get back to the question Greg and Bernard put to us a bit earlier: How much Bible content and biblical context does an unbe-

---

11 D. A. Carson, *The Gagging of God*, p. 502.

liever need to know to make a *good soil* faith response? What is the answer?" Joe was going to have the groups work on the answer at their tables, but someone shouted out, "Plenty!" right away.

"Could you elaborate?" Joe asked.

The Texan working in France answered, "Well, by telling or teaching Bible stories we give people a foundation for understanding who God is, who we are, and why Jesus had to die. By sharing those stories chronologically, we help people to connect the dots. We're finding that many of the people we meet don't know much Bible at all. What you're saying is that if we want them to understand the gospel, we need to help them know the history and concepts upon which the gospel is based."

"That's exactly right. Excellent answer. Well, there's no need to belabor this point. We're finishing a little early, but I think you all understand what we're doing. We were going to take a break and then come back for the panel on "Sharing the Gospel through Stories." Instead of going to break, let's just stand and stretch a little while the panelists come up to take their places. If we are all on the same page as I think we are, the panel shouldn't last too long and we can finish and get to the beach earlier. How does that sound?"

Cheers erupted from all over the room as people stood to stretch. After a couple of minutes of shifting around and getting the panelists seated on the platform, they were ready to continue.

"This is good. I'm ready to get to the beach again," Greg greeted the attendees as they were settling down. "Thanks so much to the Portugal team for having us. We don't have beautiful beaches in Germany like you do here. And it's so warm here. I'd like to take some of that back with me. Let me introduce our five panelists. On your left, is Jim Williams. Jim is a professional storyteller who has told Bible stories and taught missionaries in countries around the world how to tell stories effectively. Then we have Ron Jacobs from Spain, next to him, Manuel Fernandes, a local pastor from Portugal, and then you know Diana, my wife, and Miriam, Bernard's wife. Since we have been doing the majority of the leading, we thought it would be good to hear from the women. They have seen as much fruit in sharing the gospel through stories as we have. To get us

started, let's hear a brief answer from each member of the panel to this question: How have you been sharing the gospel through stories?"

The members looked at one another and smiled, not knowing who should go first.

"I'll start," said Ron Jacobs. "Awhile back I ran across a book titled *30 Days to Understanding the Bible*.[12] It's kind of like a Bible survey set up with line-art images. The idea is if you spend fifteen minutes a day reading through the book, filling in the blanks—which are like little review quizzes for each day—and using the images to remember the stories, you could understand the overarching story of the Bible in just thirty days. We adapted the idea to a teaching/storytelling mode."

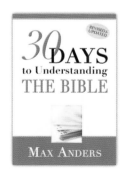

"Thanks, Ron. Manuel, what have you been doing in Portugal?"

"Well, I came to faith through a Bible panorama a missionary taught in my living room. Using cards to create a map of the Bible lands right there in the room, he almost literally walked through the Bible to give the big picture, using hand motions to help us remember the events. Then he went back and filled in the stories with more details. It was so effective in bringing me to Christ that Elisabete and I continue to use the panorama."

"Miriam and Diana, who would like to give a quick synopsis of what you're doing?"

12 Max Anders, *30 Days to Understanding the Bible* (Nashville: Nelson, 2005).

"I will," Miriam answered. "As the guys have alluded to, we are using a Bible study book that contains twenty Old Testament stories and twenty New Testament stories with a picture for each story. What we like about this tool is that it is adaptable. We can glance through it with someone reading the summary statements and looking at the pictures in twenty minutes; or we can take as many as fifty hours over several weeks reading the Bible passages and using the study questions in the booklet; or we can use a format somewhere in between."

Finally, Jim Williams spoke up. "Some of you may be thinking that since I am not ministering principally in Europe that what I have to share may not apply to your lives. I understand. But what I do I have done in many countries including some in Europe, and I have seen God bless my ministry in ways I couldn't imagine.

"What do I do? As Greg said, I am a professional storyteller. I've been telling stories—all kinds of stories—for 40 years. I used to love to tell what we in the industry call 'embellished Bible stories.' For example, instead of simply telling the story of God's testing of Abraham when He asked him to sacrifice Isaac, I would tell how Abraham thought all through the night, tossing and turning, wondering how he could ever do such a thing, agonizing over whether he would tell Sarah or not, getting up in the morning soaking wet from perspiring. All of that makes a great story, but it's all conjecture. It could have happened, but we don't have any biblical basis for it. But I have learned the power of a Bible story simply told. Now I just tell the story and watch the Holy Spirit work.

"I have developed a series called *LifeStories—True Life Stories for Living a Life that's True*. It's a set of 20 Bible events from Genesis through Revelation."

Greg addressed the assembly. "Okay, so we have some idea of what these folks are doing to reach their cultures. What questions do you have for them?"

One of the missionaries sitting down front stood up and said, "This question could be for any of you. You're all talking about quite an investment of time. Don't you get impatient? How do you wait so long to share the gospel?"

Again, the panelists looked at each other, wondering who should go first. Manuel decided to answer. "I don't know about the others, but Elisabete and I believe we are 'sharing the gospel' right from the start. We are building a base

Free Download: 🔖
www.GoodSoil.com

of biblical knowledge the unbeliever needs to know so he can believe."

"Yes," Diana added. "Tonight the guys are going to talk about our ChronoBridge at the back of *The Story of Hope*, so I don't want to steal their thunder. But some who have seen the book have said something like, 'You don't get to the gospel until the last pages!' We agree with Manuel. The gospel is all through the pages of Scripture and thus all through our book. We choose to share it chronologically in order to help people make sense of it all."

> *"… we are 'sharing the gospel' right from the start. We are building a base of biblical knowledge the unbeliever needs to know so he can believe."*

"That's right," Ron contributed. "We are sharing gospel principles right from day one of the thirty days' adaptation. It's as if we are helping put all the pieces of a puzzle together."

Another question came from the audience. "But isn't it hard to wait? Aren't you tempted to jump to Jesus' dying on the cross?"

Miriam answered, "Oh yes. Sometimes it is hard, but we fight the temptation. We could give several examples. During the lesson on Genesis 3:15 where God promises One will come to crush the serpent's head, we want to tell them Jesus is the One who came. When we tell the story of the bronze serpent, we want to tell them Jesus was also lifted up."

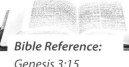

Bible Reference:
Genesis 3:15

Diana continued, "But we try to wait for at least two reasons: first, so they will have all the information they need when we get to a point of response, but also so they can make the discovery for themselves. As we go through the Old Testament stories, we obviously talk much about the sacrifices and how the lambs that died covered the sin of the people for a time, but as we saw in Genesis 3:15, God promised to send One who would be the Savior. I have then gotten to the study on John the Baptist where he declares, 'Behold the Lamb of God who takes away the sin of the world' and seen people's eyes pop. Without prompting they say, 'He's the One! Jesus is the One God promised He would send!' These are unchurched, unbelieving people, who, with the opportunity to see God's redemptive story unfold, make fantastic discoveries. How exciting it is!"

Why We Wait:
1) So they have all the information they need for a response
2) So they can make the discovery for themselves

"It sure is," Greg added from the podium. The "Amens" and the gleam in people's eyes revealed they were seeing the value in teaching Bible stories to communicate the gospel. "Any other questions?"

"How do you get someone to commit to studying the Bible with you?"

"As we get to know people, we always try to 'peel the onion' like we talked about yesterday," Diana responded. "As we do that, we get a feel for what they think about the Bible. Many times people will say something like, 'Oh, it's such a big book,' or 'It's so hard to understand,' or 'It has so many stories that don't seem to fit together.' At that point, I say, 'I have found a tool that helps to shrink the Bible down' or 'that helps me understand it,' or 'that helps to put it all together in an understandable way. Would you like to go through it with me?' Many times they will agree to a study."

"That's quite similar to what we do," added Manuel. "I'll say something like 'The Bible *can be* difficult to understand, but I have a panorama where we lay out a map right in your living room. Then we walk through the Bible so we can understand how it all fits together.'"

"You asked how we get people to study the Bible with us," storyteller Jim Williams interjected. "I don't. I invite people to a relational, storytelling time. In *LifeStories* (by the way, I have a few copies with me if you are interested in seeing it), each session starts with a story about my life; some struggle I faced yesterday or last year or 20 years ago. Or I may tell a funny story about my life or a sad story. But after I tell that story, I ask if anyone else has had a similar experience. Someone always speaks up and another, and another. After I'm convinced that we can all relate to the topic I touched on with my personal story, I say something like 'The person in our Bible story today struggled with that issue,' or 'Someone long ago also felt that way,' and I launch into the story. We're not really having a Bible study, but people are learning the Bible and applying it to their lives. And, do you want to know something really cool? Invariably, when I tell Bible stories people will look them up in the Bible. They either want to verify that the Bible actually says that or they want to know more, but Bible storytelling drives people to the Word."

"Fascinating!" Greg exclaimed.

"I have a question," came a timid voice from the right. "So is this the only way you share the gospel with people?"

Ron answered first, "Oh no, we use tracts, special events, really all kinds of things."

"We do, too," added Manuel. "But the way we have seen more people saved, discipled, and added to the church has been through interactive Bible studies such as the panorama. When we have been able to have people in our homes or go to theirs and spend significant time in the Word, God has used that to draw people to Himself."

"We have found the same thing to be true," Miriam commented. "Before we started using this tool, we saw very little lasting fruit. But consistent exposure to God's redemptive plan over an extended period of time has made a difference."

"Well, our time is about up, so if there are no more questions," Greg said and paused, "we'll go to lunch. Remember, the afternoon is open now for sightseeing and getting to the beach. We'll come back together for the evening session. Think about what you have heard today. Talk with one of the panel members if you want to learn more. We'll be glad to show you *The Story of Hope* and talk with you about how you might use Bible stories to share the gospel in your culture. Jim has some copies of *LifeStories*[13] he would be glad to show you, too. Remember, the more Bible content and biblical context you share, the better prepared your friends will be to respond in faith to Christ. See you tonight."

> *Remember, the more Bible content and biblical context you share, the better prepared your friends will be to respond in faith to Christ.*

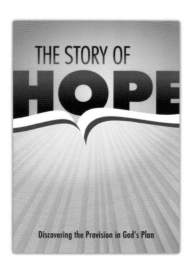

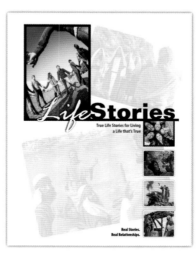

◀ *The Story of Hope* is available in several languages and formats, including a workbook and kids edition.
www.GoodSoil.com

LifeStories is a free resource available for download at *www.GoodSoil.com*

---

13 A free leader's guide for using 20 Bible events from The Story of Hope with members of the Millennials generation, as well as others which you can download here: https://www.goodsoil.com/resources/life-stories/

Part Three

HELPING *UNBELIEVERS*
EMBRACE
the Gospel

How Can We Help Them?
Our Task in the Reaping Stage

"What a beautiful day this has been!" Diana exclaimed. "We don't get November days like this in Germany."

"No we don't," Greg agreed. They had been to the beach, showered, dropped the kids off with the children's workers, and were walking hand in hand to the last meeting of the day. "But we don't have beaches like this in Germany either."

"That's right. It's been great to have this conference here in Portugal."

"Yes, but you know what's funny?" Greg asked. "I have enjoyed team teaching with Bern, and the interaction with the other missionaries has been such an encouragement—but I am itching to get back home to the ministry God gave us."

"That *is* interesting," Diana responded. "At the last two All-Western Europe Conferences we were dreading going back to Germany. Knowing that the time would end and we would have to go back to a frustrating ministry, it was almost like a dark cloud came in and hovered over the last two days. But I feel as you do. I've probably gotten more fellowship and encouragement from this conference than any other, but I am also eager to get back home."

"And have you noticed something else?" Greg asked.

"What's that?"

"We're referring to Germany as home."

As they rounded the corner to the conference room, they looked at each other and smiled with a deep sense of satisfaction. Diana squeezed his hand and asked, "Are you all set for the session tonight?"

"Let's do it!" Greg replied enthusiastically, gave her hand a return squeeze, and left her at her seat.

Tilling
Evangelism:
modeling the
Christian life,
challenging core
worldviews

Planting
Evangelism:
teaching some
gospel concepts,
establishing the
uniqueness of
Jesus

Reaping
Evangelism:
clarifying,
personalizing,
persuading,
making sure they
understand before
we look for a faith
response

"What are our roles in reaping evangelism?" Greg asked the international assembly. The group had enjoyed a good time of worship together and was settling down for the final evening session. Tomorrow morning there would be one more teaching session before they ate together and then headed to airports to spread out over the continent to resume their ministries. Greg repeated the question and then said, "I'll give you a hint. You can find the answer on the Good Soil E&D Scale. When you find the answer have your entire table stand."

It wasn't long before people at the first table were on their feet. Then two others, then some more, then the entire room was standing.

"Please be seated," Greg's voice boomed over the microphone. "Who will share one of our tasks in reaping evangelism? Just shout it out."

From the back of the room came an answer, "Clarifying."

"That's right," Greg answered with an encouraging tone. "During the tilling stage, when our audience knows very little of the gospel, we *show* them the gospel with our lives, loving them and praying for them. We also begin to challenge their core worldview. Then in the planting stage we begin to teach gospel concepts and establish the uniqueness of Jesus."

Bernard added, "We're helping them *understand* the gospel in those stages. But now in the reaping stage, one of our roles is to clarify. This is where we begin to draw in the net. What is another role of the evangelist in reaping evangelism? Someone from another table respond please."

The little Italian woman belted out, "Personalize."

"Good," Bernard continued. "When we are sure they are 'getting it,' we want to help them personalize the gospel in such a way that our unbelieving friends realize these gospel concepts are not just abstract metaphysical truths but are realities that relate personally to their lives. We want them to know they must decide what to do with Jesus Christ. We will talk about how we do that in a moment. But first, what is our other role in reaping evangelism?"

A missionary to Spain who had been the conference jester (There is always at least one.) lifted his voice in a mock preaching style and said, "We must persuade them. Can I get an amen?" Then he added, "*Persuade*," saying it as if it were a word with four syllables.

After the chuckles died down, Greg responded, still smiling and trying to match his style, "Exactly, brother." Then he continued more seriously. "In the reaping stage we *do* need to appropriately persuade the unbeliever to turn from whatever he has trusted in for spiritual hope and to put his trust

in Jesus Christ for the forgiveness of sins and receive God's gift of eternal life. In 2 Corinthians 5:11, Paul said, 'Therefore, knowing the fear of the Lord, we persuade others.' Persuading unbelievers to trust Christ is a biblical concept. In some cultures however, we must be careful about using human persuasion. Many people feel compelled to go along with anything that a respected person asks them to do, even though they may not understand what they are doing or may not be acting from their hearts. And, of course, we do not want to usurp the work of the Holy Spirit. *He* is the true Persuader. But as we seek to clarify the gospel for people and help them to personalize it, we ought not shy away from gently persuading them to trust Christ as Savior."

Bible Reference:
2 Corinthians 5:11

"Notice on the Good Soil Scale," Bernard cut in, "that this is where an unbeliever accepts or embraces the gospel. A Good Soil person first understands the gospel and then makes it his own. Remember the Greek word *paradechomai* means to receive with open arms, welcome or embrace. That is why our tasks at the reaping stage are so important. Unbelievers who do not embrace the gospel and make it their own will either never trust Christ or they will fall by the wayside. Our clarifying, personalizing, and persuading are all part of the divine-human cooperative of evangelism."

> *Clarifying, personalizing, and persuading are all part of the divine-human cooperative of evangelism in the reaping stage.*

Bernard continued: "We have developed a tool for this stage of evangelism specifically to help us fulfill those three roles. We call it the *Chronological Bridge to Life*, or ChronoBridge for short, and have put it in the back of our book *The Story of Hope*. We could tell how we think the tool helps us fulfill those roles, but we'd rather have you interact with the tool and discover on your own how it might be a help in your ministry. So we have made a copy of one of the two-page spreads for you to work on. Four two-page spreads make up the ChronoBridge. On each spread, we deal with two of the eight Essential Truths.

1 God   3 Sin   5 Christ   7 Faith
2 Man   4 Death   6 Cross   8 Life

The two-page spread you have will deal only with two of these essentials. At your tables, read through the spread and answer these questions: How do you think the ChronoBridge helps to *clarify*? How do you think the Chrono-Bridge helps to *personalize*? How do you think the ChronoBridge helps to *persuade*? You'll have 15 minutes to do this."

God

What we have learned about our Creator:

1. The God of the Bible has always existed and will continue to exist forever. Because He is eternal, God referred to Himself as the "I AM" (Yahweh or Jehovah) which is translated in our Bibles as LORD.
2. By simply commanding it into existence, God created the world and everything in it. In its original condition, God's creation was perfect.
3. Throughout the Bible, this Creator-God continually demonstrated that He is all-powerful.

4. In contrast with false gods, the true God is perfectly holy (totally without sin).
5. As the Creator of mankind, God gave men and women clear commands to obey.
6. God is a righteous and fair Judge who must and will punish disobedience.
7. God loves us even when we disobey Him.

Which of these truths about God would you like to understand better?
Circle one or more numbers.

God   Man   Sin   Death

SPIRITUAL DEATH

1

The Bible says: *But without faith it is impossible to please Him, for he who comes to God must believe that He is, and that He is a rewarder of those who diligently seek Him.* (Hebrews 11:6)

Our Faith Response: From the Bible we learn that one, and only one, true eternal and holy God exists, that He is our all-powerful Creator and just Judge, and that we are accountable to Him. Do you believe this?

Man

What we have learned about mankind:

1. Human beings (people) are uniquely created by God, in His image. As such, we were given some qualities and abilities which God's other creatures did not receive.
2. These special qualities and abilities equip us to be caretakers of God's creation, a role that God has assigned to us.
3. God loves all human beings and desires that we be in perfect fellowship with Him and enjoy His presence.

4. Not only did God give us the responsibility and ability to obey Him, He also gave us the capacity to disobey.
5. Because God made us and owns us, every human being is accountable to Him.
6. Human beings were created with a material body as well as an immaterial spirit.
7. The spirit of man will never cease to exist; it will live forever in a resurrected body.

Which of these truths about mankind would you like to understand better?
Circle one or more numbers.

Christ   Cross   Faith   Life

ETERNAL LIFE

2

The Bible says: *And the LORD God formed man of the dust of the ground, and breathed into his nostrils the breath of life; and man became a living being.* (Genesis 2:7)

Our Faith Response: From the Bible we learn that we are made by God, loved by God, and that God deserves our full obedience. Do you believe this?

Exercise #15:

One of the two-page spreads is reproduced on the previous page spread for you. Read through it and answer the questions yourself before going on.

*How do you think the ChronoBridge helps to **clarify**?*

*How do you think the ChronoBridge helps to **personalize**?*

*How do you think the ChronoBridge helps to **persuade**?*

"Time is up," Greg spoke over the public address system. "How did you do? Someone give us one way in which the bridge helps to clarify."

Ron Jacobs, who seemed to be the natural leader at his table, was quick to respond. "From the two pages we have, it looks like there are seven statements dealing with 'what we've learned' for each of the essential truths. These statements are clear, concise summaries of biblical truth related to each of the essential truths."

"Thank you for that response," Greg answered. "There *are* seven for each truth, which if you multiply seven times eight, gives you fifty-six truths. Something you might be interested to know is that each of the fifty-six truths comes directly out of one or more of the Bible stories that make up *The Story of Hope*. So when we say 'what we have learned about our Creator … mankind,' etc., we are being literal. These are truths we have learned as we worked through the Bible stories. On the ChronoBridge pages they are stated clearly in summary form."

One of the participants on the left raised a hand. "Yes?" Greg acknowledged.

"We also thought that the specific Bible verse dealing with the essential truth included on each page helps to clarify those truths for an unbeliever."

"Very good," replied Greg. "Having a reference right there on the page is helpful, isn't it? Anyone else? Anything else that clarifies?"

The youth worker from Luxembourg raised his hand tentatively. Greg called on him, and he spoke up, "Well, at this table we realized that Our Faith Response on each page is there to help *personalize* the truths, but we also saw it as a clarifier. I mean, if the seven statements up above summarize the truths gained from the Bible stories, then the faith response summarizes the seven into one succinct statement. Don't you think?"

Bernard was already standing as the youth worker finished speaking, and Greg offered him the microphone. "Yes, we do think. That's a great observation because it's exactly what Greg was trying to do as he put these pages together. In the faith responses we have taken what we have learned in the Bible stories and distilled it into eight affirmations of Bible truth. Good work. Your observation also serves as a good transition to the

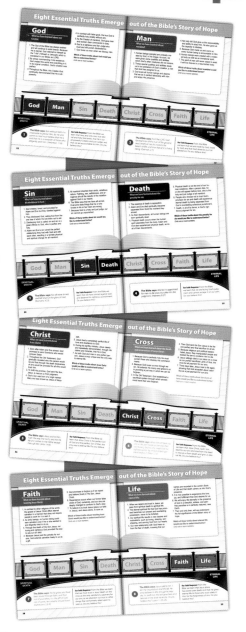

ChronoBridge:

Clarifies:
*gives 56 biblical
truths, provides a
clear Bible verse,
summarizes into a
clear faith response*

Personalizes:
*asks "Do you
believe this?" and
asks about which
truths they would
like to understand
better*

next question. Our Faith Response does personalize because after every statement the question is directed toward the student: 'Do you believe this?'"

"You can't get much more personal than that!" the Luxembourg leader interjected.

"No you can't," agreed Bernard. "What else did you find that helps to personalize, class?"

Miriam interrupted, "I'm sorry, Bern, could I just say something about the faith response before you go on?"

"Certainly, *liebling.*"

"I just wanted to say that Our Faith Response has been a great tool within a tool for me. First of all, 'our faith response' is in the plural, which makes it less threatening, I think. It isn't just directed to the reader, but includes me and any others who are exposed to the book. That in itself helps the reader be less defensive. But I also like having the question 'Do you believe this?' right there in print. For me just to look someone in the eye and ask a question like that is a little scary. But since it is written in the book, I can read it and ask them in a less intimidating manner. It's not just *my* idea, so it's easier for me to confront people. I've seen time after time the importance of that confrontation. It makes people grapple with the significance of the gospel for their own lives."

"*Danke*, Miri," said Bern. "I'm so glad you shared that from your personal experience. Any other observations on how the ChronoBridge personalizes?"

The college student from Ireland stood and Bernard acknowledged him. He spoke in his distinct brogue. "The question that starts with 'which of these truths about' and ends with 'would you like to understand better?' on each page is also helpful to personalize. Our group thought that if we *don't* ask that question or something similar, it would be 'beyond the pale.'"

Bernard and Greg asked at the same time, "Excuse me?"

"Oh, sorry," the Irish student replied. "'Beyond the pale' is a phrase used in Ireland and many other places, too, which means it is unacceptable or unreasonable. We felt that as we share the gospel, if we don't ask if people understand or what they would like to understand better, it would be 'beyond the pale'—unacceptable. The least we can do is to make sure they understand the gospel. And as you blokes have pointed out, asking if they understand personalizes the truths as well."

"Thank you, Patrick," Bernard replied. "We all learned a new phrase today, too. I'm going to talk with Pat later to learn the etymology of that phrase. Well, class, the time is flying. What about persuading? How does the ChronoBridge help to persuade?"

An intense Portuguese pastor with a serious look on his face lifted his hand and asked, "*Posso?*"

Bernard, who had vacationed twice in Portugal and understood a smattering of Portuguese, showed off his Portuguese, "*Faz favor*, go right ahead."

Alberto, a Portuguese pastor, who understood English very well but had difficulty expressing himself in English, said, "*A minha esposa vai traduzir.*"

Then his wife stood and said in clear English with just a hint of an accent, "He would like me to translate." For the next several minutes, the pastor spoke a sentence, then his wife repeated it in English, and so it continued. Here is a summary: "This is an excellent tool for evangelism. I am so glad you have developed it. I think it will be very effective in Portugal, so we would like to translate it into Portuguese. You asked us how the ChronoBridge persuades. I believe the very way the pages are set up will help to convince. You have several biblical affirmations listed that have grown out of Bible stories already read. It is as if the statements are building an argument. Then there is a verse that reiterates the truth. Then the faith response summarizes that truth and asks for a response. These pages naturally persuade the reader of the truth of the gospel. Thank you for your hard work on this."

"Well, thank *you* for your kind words," Bernard responded humbly, head down. "We have found this tool to be very effective and hope others can use it, also. We will make it available to be translated for whoever would like it. Before we finish for the evening, we have one more exercise we would like you all to do. We hope others can use *The Story of Hope*, but we aren't so naïve to think that it will work everywhere or in exactly the same way. With that in mind, we believe there is a lot of flexibility in the tool, even in using the ChronoBridge. Here is what we would like you to do now: Discuss different ways in which the Bridge could be used. Just because it is in print on these pages does not mean that it must be presented in this format. Be creative and try to think of different ways in which the *material* on these pages could be shared with a friend in your context and culture."

Persuades:
Biblical statements build an argument, verse reiterates the truth, faith response summarizes truth

Different Ways of Sharing the ChronoBridge

- The presenter (evangelist) could read (and possibly supply a brief explanation of) the seven summary points and then ask the recipient to identify one or more of these truths that he did not understand clearly.

- The presenter could ask the recipient to read these points silently and then identify points where clarification is needed.

- The presenter could read the odd-numbered points (aloud) and ask the recipient to read the even-numbered points, etc.

- If the recipient is willing to do so, the presenter could ask the recipient to study pages 32-39 before coming to the Bible study session and ask him to identify (prior to the meeting) the points that need to be clarified.

- The presenter could lead the recipient in a discussion regarding where these gospel concepts appeared in the events in the chronological Bible story on pages 12-31.

- The ChronoBridge could be presented while flipping through the Bible, referring to the actual stories.

- The presenter could flip through pages 12-32, pointing to the pictures of particular stories that are relevant to the truths of the ChronoBridge being mentioned.

- The presenter could draw a bridge and symbols representing the 8 truths (God, Man, Sin, Death, Christ, Cross, Faith, Life) as she walks through the ChronoBridge material.

Exercise #16:

Can you think of any other ways to share the ChronoBridge?

Find the ChronoBridge on the free mobile app at: www.GoodSoil.com/Hope-c-app

The Story of Hope
visual mobile app

After several minutes of discussion in small groups, then sharing with the large group, the conference-goers had a list (see previous page) on a flip chart that Diana and Miriam recorded as they were given.

Joe ascended the platform and asked, "Hasn't this been an enlightening time for us?" The participants started applauding right away. After a few seconds of normal applause, the whole group began to clap in concert: *clap … clap … clap … clap*, in unison slowly at first and then speeding up until it sounded like normal applause again, showing in European fashion that the seminar was very much appreciated.

Joe continued, "Thank you so much, Bern and Miriam and Greg and Diana. I believe God has begun to do something great through you in Germany. We are glad this tool He provided can be used all over Europe—maybe even the world."

Now addressing the entire audience, Joe continued, "But we have arrived at the challenge of the week for us all, Euro Team. Bern and Greg showed us *The Story of Hope* they have developed and used effectively to help unbelievers truly understand, then embrace the gospel. But do you remember the third emphasis we learned from the Parable of the Soils?"

"Retain or hold it fast, wasn't it?" the Belgian pastor asked. "In Luke's version we saw that the *good soil* person retains the gospel."

"That's right. Thank you," Joe replied. "And how do we ensure that people retain the gospel?"

Not sure that anyone would answer his rhetorical question, Joe paused for effect anyway. But then someone did respond. It was an elderly gentleman from France who had been faithfully pastoring for years with little or no help. Missionaries had come and gone, usually not staying long, but this diminutive *vieil homme* had stayed the course for over 50 years. He spoke in a voice that didn't seem to fit so much with his short stature but more with his patriarchal role and said simply, slowly, "Follow-up."

Vieil homme:
French, "old man"

"Thank you, sir," Joe humbly acknowledged his senior in ministry. "That, along with more extensive discipleship, is exactly what I had in mind. When people place their trust in Christ as Savior, immediate follow-up is necessary to begin to ground them in their faith. Then we must continue to disciple and mentor people throughout their faith journey. After all, Jesus commissioned us to *make disciples*. Greg and Bern have developed this great tool for evangelism that we can translate for our work. Many of you are already using other creative, effective methods. But here in Europe, and possibly all around the world, our mission is weak in discipleship. Our task tomorrow is to come up with a comprehensive plan or strategy for discipleship that could be adapted and used all over Europe. So enjoy each other's company for the rest of the evening, get some rest tonight, and come back in the morning ready to contribute something that might help us all fulfill the task Jesus gave us."

Looking toward the French patriarch, Joe asked, "Brother, could you please come to the mic and close this time in prayer?"

The veteran pastor walked slowly to the platform. Joe gave him a hand-held microphone because he probably would not have been heard from behind the podium.

"*Merci, Pasteur* Joseph," he nodded to Joe with tears in his eyes. Then with a strong but understandable accent he addressed Joe and the crowd. "We are grateful for this conference. God took me to Africa as a missionary for 23 years, to North America where I pastored for 10 years, and now back to France for these past 19 years where I have been planting a church in Annecy. God, to whom belongs all praise and glory, has graciously blessed our ministry on each continent. Amen, alleluia, amen. But I can see how *The Story of Hope* could have helped tremendously to bring people to the Savior in each place where we ministered, especially in this *âge postmoderne*. May God bless this tool and others that may be developed for His glory." He then launched into a prayer for Europe and when he finished there was not a dry eye left in the house.

Part Four

HELPING *BELIEVERS*

RETAIN

the Gospel

Then What?
What We Can Do to Preserve the Fruit

"You know, Diana," Greg observed as they walked to the final morning of the conference, "I kind of feel lighter today now that our teaching responsibilities are over. It's going to be fun to sit and participate without having to be concerned with what's coming next and whether I'm ready or not."

Just then they rounded the corner of the hotel hallway opening into the conference room area and stopped short. The atrium was filled with people. The delegates—foreign missionaries, local pastors, and international workers—were all milling around. No one had entered the auditorium.

"What's up?" Greg asked the first person he saw. It was Patrick, the student leader from Ireland.

"There's a sign on the door of the conference room asking us to wait out here," he replied. Then with a grin, he asked, "Well, boy?" The day before Patrick had been teaching Greg some Irish phrases. Now he wanted to see how well Greg would remember.

Greg faked a grimace and held his stomach, saying, "*Cat malogan*, I think it was the *red lead* from yesterday's lunch. Well, *butty*?"

They both laughed heartily as Diana just looked on, bewildered.

"Now ye're talkin'!" Patrick complimented Greg. "Ye can come to Ireland anytime."

Greg had pity on his wife and told her about the conversation and lesson from the day before. He finished, "So with 'well, boy' he asked me how I was doing. I told him I was terrible. I thought it was from the luncheon sausage I ate yesterday, and asked how he was doing."

Diana just shook her head and smiled. She might have had a witty comeback, but Joe was waving his hands and asking for everyone's attention.

"Good morning, everyone. Thanks for waiting. Before you walk through the double doors into the meeting room, we want you to find everyone from the country where you minister—internationals or locals—and form a unit. Then, respond as a group to the questions on these papers I am handing out. When you do go in, sit together. Does anyone have any questions?"

"What are we working on?" someone shouted from the middle of the crowd.

"The questions on the paper deal with discipleship. We want to hear what you are doing and what you think you need," Joe responded. "If there are no other questions, form your groups and jump in. You have half an hour."

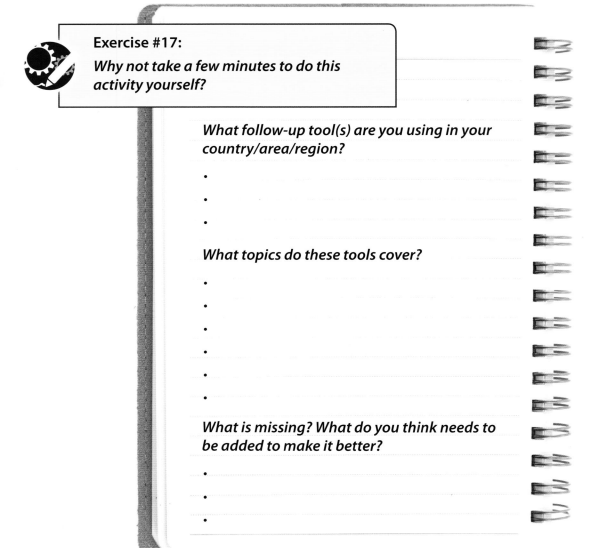

Exercise #17:

Why not take a few minutes to do this activity yourself?

What follow-up tool(s) are you using in your country/area/region?

- •
- •
- •

What topics do these tools cover?

- •
- •
- •
- •
- •

What is missing? What do you think needs to be added to make it better?

- •
- •
- •

"Thanks for your hard work and interaction on this topic," Joe began when the groups reassembled. "When I first took this job as administrator of Western Europe, I didn't think discipleship would be an issue because it is such a vital part of mission work. I expected people would naturally be involved in discipling. But I soon learned few of us are doing discipleship in a regular, consistent manner. When I talked with other administrators I found they have seen weaknesses in follow-up as well. What really opened my eyes was the survey new missionary appointees filled in last year. Only 10 percent said they had discipled an adult in a methodical way. Since we are seeking to carry out the entire Great Commission, we should get a better handle on making *disciples* of all nations. I noticed as you were working on the assignment none of you were really excited about the material you are presently using, if you are doing anything at all! So I would like you to come up with subjects you think should be covered in a basic follow-up tool for use when someone comes to Christ. What does he or she need to know? What biblical instruction is necessary for growth at this stage? Take ten minutes to formulate your list. Then travel as a unit to the other flip charts and read what others have written. As you do this, put a green mark on the subjects your group did *not* include that you now recognize as important. Put a red mark by topics you think could be left out at this level. In this way we should get a pretty good idea of what two hundred Christian workers think should be included in an initial follow-up tool. Begin."

At the end of ten minutes each group had listed at least seven topics; some had as many as fifteen. Then they began visiting each other's charts for two minutes each, moving in a clockwise direction. Laughter and chatter filled the room for the next twenty minutes as the exercise took its course. When the groups returned to their tables, Joe asked for a response.

Greg spoke up. "At times we jokingly picked on a group; at times we were amazed at the insight displayed by listing a topic that made so much sense but we had left off our list. I appreciated what each group had to say."

"Good," Joe thanked him. "You all have done a great job. As I look around the room, I see some definite patterns emerging. Let's take a twenty-minute break during which I will ask the German team to help me organize these lists. See you in twenty."

Greg and Diana worked with Bernard, Miriam, and Joe to compile the lists and put together a possible table of contents for a follow-up study. Then they prepared the data projector and put the Good Soil E&D Scale on the screen for the closing session.

∂∂Q∂∂

After the break, a singing group representing eight of the countries in attendance opened the meeting with a chorus.

So let's tell the world of Jesus, of His love,
Tell them of His promises, of heaven above.
We must go and tell them, obeying His plan for us.
We must tell the world of Jesus.[14]

"Thank you, Manuel, for leading the group in that beautiful reminder that we all are part of God's plan for reaching the nations. Notice on the Good Soil E&D Scale on the screen that helping believers to grow is included in that plan. Earlier we saw how *The Story of Hope* can be used to help unbelievers understand and embrace the gospel. But our task is not finished until we help them … what's the word?"

> *Our task in evangelism and discipleship is not finished until we help people hold fast to the gospel.*

Almost in unison, the crowd shouted, "Hold fast to the gospel."

"That's right. Notice how Matthew 13:23 moves through Tilling Evangelism and Planting Evangelism. That's where we help unbelievers understand the gospel. Mark 4:20 covers Reaping Evangelism where we help unbelievers embrace the gospel. After the faith response, we help believers hold fast to the gospel. That's the word used in Luke 8:15. Unbelievers start at -12 and move up the scale through decreasingly negative numbers until they get to zero, 'repents and trusts Jesus.' Then we see increasingly positive numbers that represent growth in Christ. Someone please read 2 Corinthians 1:24 for us."

Bible References:
Matthew 13:23
Mark 4:20
Luke 8:15
2 Corinthians 1:24

Ron Jacobs found the passage quickly and read, "Not that we lord it over your faith, but we work with you for your joy, for you stand firm in your faith."

"Thanks, Ron," Joe continued. "This is a disciple-maker's verse. This idea of standing firm by faith is similar to retaining, keeping one's faith. Paul is saying that when we teach disciples, helping them to stand firm in their faith and retain the gospel, it is for their joy. It is not to be bossy or pushy or to show we know more than they do, but to lead them down a path to joy. I think we'll call this follow-up tool you are helping to create *The Way to Joy*. If we can help establish people in the faith they will keep for a lifetime and forever, we will lead them in the way to joy. I'm excited about the Table of Contents we can show you from the compiled lists you produced. I'll put it up on the screen as the guys pass out copies.

Basic Steps in Following Jesus

THE WAY TO
JOY

Pursuing Basic Steps to Discipleship

Lesson 1: *The Joy of Hope:*   *God's Eternal Plan*
Lesson 2: *The Joy of Eternal Life:*   *Salvation*
Lesson 3: *The Joy of Confidence:*   *Assurance and Security*
Lesson 4: *The Joy of Guidance:*   *God's Word*
Lesson 5: *The Joy of Communion:*   *Prayer*
Lesson 6: *The Joy of Empowerment:* *The Spirit-Controlled Life*
Lesson 7: *The Joy of Purity:*   *Personal Holiness*
Lesson 8: *The Joy of Sharing:*   *Witnessing*
Lesson 9: *The Joy of Fellowship:*   *The Local Church*
Lesson 10: *The Joy of Purpose:*   *God's Plan for You*

Available from: 🔖
www.GoodSoil.com

"As you might guess by looking at the title, the first lesson will be a review of God's redemptive plan as we saw in *The Story of Hope*. Bernard and Greg have already developed a twenty-story version that will serve nicely as a review for those who have gone through *The Story of Hope* and made a faith response. It can also be used with a new believer who did *not* go through *The Story of Hope* to help her see the significance of God's big story. Lesson two will be a review of the ChronoBridge to Life, to help solidify a faith response from someone who has never seen the ChronoBridge. Greg, can we put the top half of the Good Soil E&D Scale up on the screen?" *(appears on the next page in this book)* Greg clicked to the next slide. "Pursuing Basic Steps to Discipleship" appeared on the screen. "Thanks. Now look at the lesson topics and compare them with the top half of the scale. Lesson three will deal with Assurance and Security. With which line on the scale does that correspond?"

Someone simply said, "The 'plus 2' line."

"Right," continued Joe. "And Lessons 4 and 5 will teach the importance of Bible study and prayer which correspond with which step on the scale?"

Another answered, "The next step up."

"Exactly, and this will continue throughout *The Way to Joy*, each lesson dealing with the next area of growth on the scale. Does anyone see any problem with that?"

The quiet pastor from Belgium hesitantly raised his hand, and Joe nodded to him. "I'm not sure I see a problem, it's just that not everyone grows in the same way or passes through these steps in the same order."

"You're right!" Joe replied. "I was hoping someone might point that out. Everyone turn your paper over now and take a moment to look at the growth scale. On the right-hand side of the Luke 8:15 arrow you see a ladder with the word *You* at the top. Silently, there at your seat, think through your growth as a new believer and list the order in which you saw those steps of growth in your own life. Put a '1' by the phrase that describes what happened first in your life, a '2' by what happened second, etc."

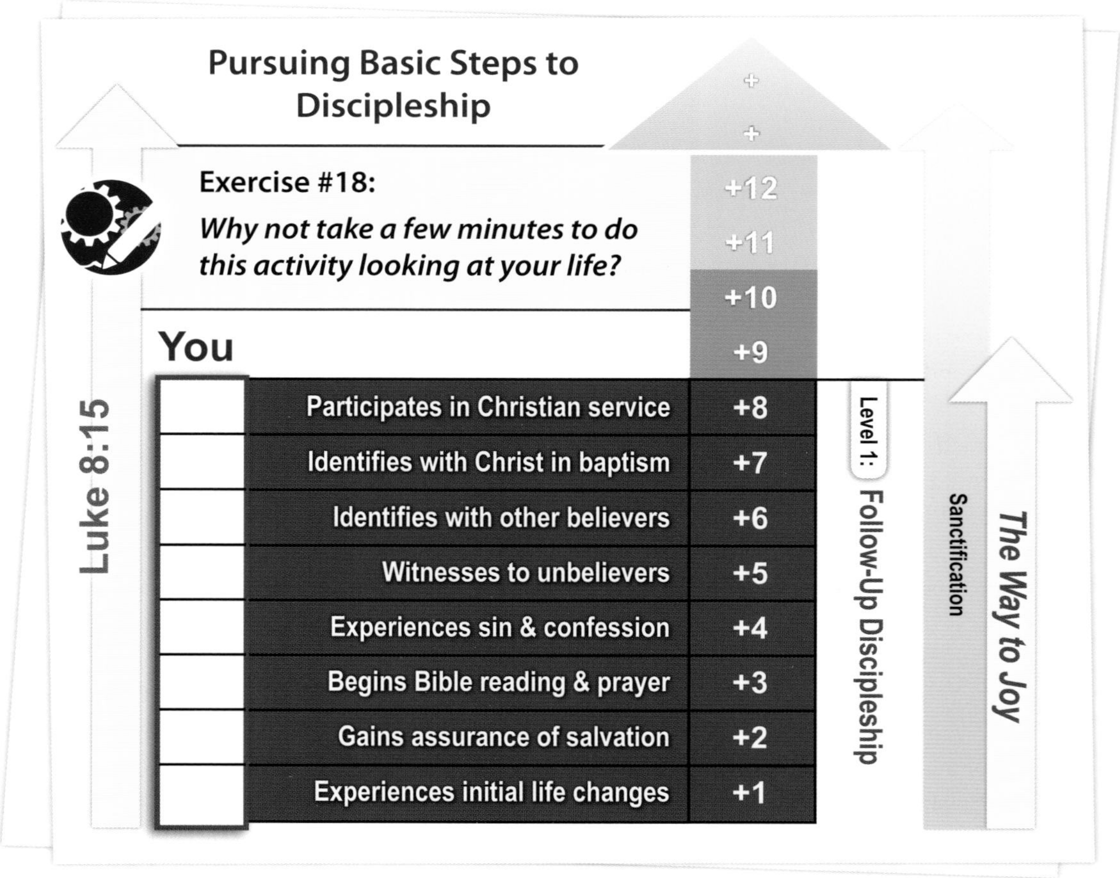

Pursuing Basic Steps to Discipleship

Exercise #18:

Why not take a few minutes to do this activity looking at your life?

You

	Participates in Christian service	+8
	Identifies with Christ in baptism	+7
	Identifies with other believers	+6
	Witnesses to unbelievers	+5
	Experiences sin & confession	+4
	Begins Bible reading & prayer	+3
	Gains assurance of salvation	+2
	Experiences initial life changes	+1

+12
+11
+10
+9

Luke 8:15

Level 1: Follow-Up Discipleship

Sanctification

The Way to Joy

The group worked quietly for a couple of minutes. When the majority was looking up or talking softly, Joe addressed them again.

"Okay now, I'm going to read my numbers in order from bottom to top while you look at your column and compare it to mine. Ready? 6, 4, 3, 1, 5, 2, 7, 8. Whoever has the exact same order please stand."

No one in the room stood.

"Anyone?"

No one moved.

"Hmmph," Joe feigned disappointment. "Well, someone else read the numbers in your ladder starting at the bottom and going to the top. If someone has the exact order please stand."

Greg's new friend Patrick read loudly, "2, 4, 5, 3, 1, 7, 6, 8."

The young Castilian pastor jumped to his feet and cheered, "*Soy yo!*" Nearly everyone laughed.

Soy yo:
That's me!

Joe, regaining his own composure, asked, "Anyone else match Patrick's list?" Scanning the auditorium for raised hands, Joe commented, "Okay, one or two. You see, in a group this big, we are bound to find a few that show similar patterns, but the point is that we have different experiences. We will not all grow at the same rate, in the same way, or even experience the same order of growth steps. This means we can use a tool like this in a variety of ways. We can use it as is, covering lessons one through ten in order. Or we can cover lessons different from the printed order as we see fit for the person with whom we are working. Let's turn back to the Table of Contents. I would like the following people to come and stand across the front of the auditorium: Bernard and Miriam, Greg and Diana from Germany, Patrick from Ireland, Ron from Spain, Pastor Lemont from Belgium, Manuel and Andreia from Portugal, and Sofia *de Italia.*"

Bernard, Miriam, Greg, and Diana were already sitting up front so they stood and turned around. They saw vibrant Patrick jump from his seat and practically run down the aisle. They also saw the French patriarch rise slowly from his seat and arrive at the front after the others. Joe waited patiently and continued only after the group was all assembled.

Addressing the entire audience, he said, "You didn't realize it, but we did a lot of work on that last break. The people standing here have agreed to work on this project and try to have *The Way to Joy* written, revised, and printed by the beginning of next year. We have chosen people from six different countries who already have a significant ministry in evangelism and discipleship.

Available from: 🔖
www.GoodSoil.com

Obviously, others of you could have been on the team as well, but we had to limit the number. We want to pray for the team as they develop this new tool. They will then head up translation teams in their countries. We will get others involved as needed so we can have this follow-up tool available across our region. Let's pray now for our colleagues that God will guide and help them as they begin to write *The Way to Joy* for His glory."

The group in front joined hands as several in the auditorium led in prayer. As they prayed, Greg was moved deeply. He thought back just a couple of years ago when he was seeing so little fruit that he was sure he had made a mistake and did not belong on the mission field. He thanked God for his team and the way He had led them in developing *The Story of Hope* to communicate His redemptive plan in worldview-appropriate ways.

And now he was part of the team who would write a discipleship tool. He glanced over at Pastor Pierre Lemont, the French patriarch. What a privilege it would be to work with and learn from this faithful man of God!

Beyond Pastor Lemont was his "linguistics teacher" Patrick. Greg smiled as he imagined the fun Patrick would bring to the table, but he could also see Patrick's fiery devotion to God and passion for people.

There was the Portuguese couple God was using in unique ways, and Jacobs from Spain, and the feisty Italian lady, and the foursome. Greg was confident God would use this group, and he was humbled yet honored to be a part of it. The final "Amen" brought him back to the room, and he whispered, "Amen. Thank you, Lord. Use us for Your glory, and may these resources help to make disciples throughout Europe and around the world."

Epilogue

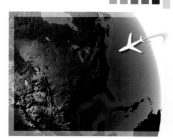

The plane jostled its passengers a bit, and the seat-belt light came on with a ding. Greg stood, steadied himself, and checked the seat belts on his sleeping children. He and Diana were enjoying silence during the last couple of hours of their eight-hour Frankfurt/New York flight. After transferring in New York, they still had another flight to Grandma and Grandpa's house where they would start their ministry of reporting to churches and sharing what God was doing in their lives.

"Can you believe they're finally asleep?" he whispered to Diana.

"Whew!" she responded. "It took awhile, but they finally zonked out. I hope they get some rest. They'll need it. By the time we get to bed it will be well into tomorrow morning Frankfurt time. It's a long day for them."

"They'll be fine," Greg comforted. "Young bodies bounce back quickly. I'm more concerned about this old body!"

"Oh, you'll be fine," Diana said in a pampering voice and squeezed his cheek as she would a child. Then pensively she added, "My hero will be fine."

"Hero?" Greg asked. "What's this? You never talk that way."

Diana turned so she could face Greg and sandwiched his hand in hers. "I know, but you are my hero. You were convinced we should leave Germany, but you let God speak to you when Bern and Miri challenged us. Then you helped create *The Story of Hope* and after that *The Way to Joy*. Now you plan on working with others to develop the second- and third-level discipleship materials." She paused and with brimming eyes said in a low voice, "Thanks for being open to God's leading and for being my example."

Greg could feel the heat rising from his neck as he blushed at Diana's words. "Thanks," he said softly. "God has done a work in both of us, hasn't He? We wanted to leave and never come back, and now I wish we didn't have to leave. We're still in the air headed to the States, and already I can't wait to get back to Germany! Our ministry may not be what people call flourishing yet, but it is steadily growing. And it's all because of Good Soil E&D."

"Yep. The theology of evangelism and discipleship that came out of our study has certainly changed the way we do ministry. The church in Frankfurt is growing, and we have so many friends—believers and unbelievers—in whom God is working that I, too, wish we didn't have to leave. But I'm excited about peeling onions and using *The Story of Hope* with people we will meet in America this year."

"Me, too. Let's commit always to be ready to initiate conversations that may become redemptive relationships wherever we are."

Cultivate

"Want-to-Be Wiccan" Makes a Faith-Change

Moriah attended an Easter service with her fiancé in a southern US state. After the service, Moriah met the pastor in the lobby of the church. She said, "I need to let you know I don't believe the same as you do. I'm looking to become a Wiccan." Later, the pastor asked Moriah and her fiancé to participate in a Bible study, using *The Story of Hope*. The study continued for several weeks, but Moriah could not get past Jesus' declaration in John 5 that He was "equal to and one with God the Father." In the next lesson, the study focused on John 11 and Martha's faith response, "I believe that you are the Christ, the Son of God." After consulting with her fiancé's Christian grandfather, Moriah too responded in faith to Jesus and the gospel.

Read the full stories and more at www.GoodSoil.com/Blog

Chinese PhD Now Understands the Big Story

Heng, a PhD graduate and professor of engineering, and his wife Lan are from China but live in South Africa. As an intellectually honest agnostic, Heng had read the entire Bible but only saw it as a bunch of disconnected stories. When a missionary pastor led Heng and Lan through a study using *The Way to Joy*, at the end of lesson one Heng commented, "Now, it all makes sense. It's really one Big Story." At the end of lesson two, Lan wept and put her faith in Jesus. A few weeks later, Heng came to the study and said, "I now have the faith to believe."

Jesus Christ Fills Gloria's Spiritual Vacuum

Growing up in Spain, Gloria's parents were teachers of Roman Catholicism and her grandfather was a priest. But, at age 13, she began to sense a spiritual vacuum that the Church was not filling. A few years later, her friend Cody encouraged her to read the Bible and attend an evangelical church. During a study through *The Story of Hope*, Gloria began to understand God's gracious plan of redemption and placed her faith in Jesus as her Savior. Gloria continued her growth in faith through studying *The Way to Joy*.

Nepalese and "The Scars of Easter"

The Hindu beliefs of many Nepalese make it difficult for them to understand and embrace many biblical truths about Jesus, especially the nature of His unique "God in flesh" incarnation and His bodily resurrection from the dead. Ministering to a Nepalese community in Hong Kong, a missionary used *The Story of Hope* teaching visuals to present an Easter sermon that he called "The Scars of Easter." He unfolded the Bible's redemptive story line from Genesis through Revelation, reinforcing the key events using the high-quality visuals. When he showed the visual of the postresurrection scars in Jesus' hands, they "got it." Eight Nepalese trusted Jesus as Savior that day.

Buddhist Finds the Answer He Sought

Growing up in a country that restricts missionary activity, Linh was firmly indoctrinated by his Buddhist mother and grandparents. But he agreed to study *The Story of Hope* with a Christ-follower who was living in the country on a non-missionary visa. Linh's mother and grandparents told him that this Bible man was up to no good, so Linh quit coming to the study. But he could not escape the haunting question he had heard in the study: "What is the purpose of life?" His grandparents, many other highly esteemed people, and even the Buddhist priest at the Pagoda could not give him the answer. Finally, the grandparents advised him to go back to the Bible man to learn the answer. After a thorough study of *The Story of Hope*, Linh found his answer in Jesus.

The Story of Hope in a Ukrainian Village

A missionary doctor visited a remote and poor Ukrainian village with a Ukrainian pastor once a month in order to provide medical care and share God's story of hope with them. Initially, the villagers were hesitant to learn about anything that contradicted their Russian Orthodox works-based religion. But after a few months, some of them agreed to participate in a Bible study using the Russian translation of *The Story of Hope*. Even though the villagers had grown up in the Russian Orthodox Church, they knew very little about the Bible and were soon captivated by the Bible's redemptive story. A core group of villagers remained faithful to the study for several months and, at the conclusion of the study, four of them placed their faith in Jesus Christ.

Good Soil Seminar

If you have enjoyed learning about Good Soil Evangelism and Discipleship along with Greg, Diana, Bern, and Miriam, we invite you to master these principles more deeply by participating in a Good Soil seminar.

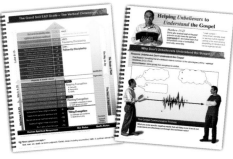
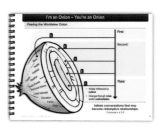

In the seminar, learn how to …

- *Evaluate* a person's spiritual status on the Good Soil Evangelism and Discipleship Scale.
- Peel an unbeliever's "worldview onion" through casual conversations.
- *Determine* how much gospel content and Biblical context an unbeliever needs in order to make a *good soil* faith response.
- *Penetrate* unbiblical "worldview noise" using God's redemptive story, as it unfolds from Genesis through Revelation.
- Use the *Chronological Bridge to Life* to help unbelievers embrace the gospel of Jesus Christ.
- *Disciple* new believers through their first steps in following Jesus.

Become equipped to use …

Good Soil Basic Seminar

- Two days of interactive training.
- Includes lunch, snacks, and instructional materials.
- Includes the *Good Soil Seminar Workbook, The Story of Hope, The Way to Joy, Gaining Ground with Good Soil,* and *The Story of Hope—Condensed.*

Good Soil Trainer Certification Workshop

- Additional *(and optional)* day of training to equip and certify trainers to lead Good Soil Basic Seminars.
- Includes *Training Wheels for Good Soil Trainers* (instructor's guide for leading a Good Soil Basic Seminar), lunch, and snacks.

Good Soil training is offered every May and October at ABWE, near Harrisburg, PA. www.GoodSoil.com/Training

Resources

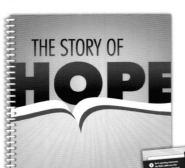

The Story of Hope
Discovering the Provision in God's Plan

A time-flexible tool for presenting the Bible's redemptive story in as few as fifteen minutes or as long as twenty or more hours. Designed for evangelistic Bible studies but also helpful in teaching the Bible's Big Story to believers.

Free Leader's Guides Available

- **The Story of Hope Leader's Guide** contains 103 professionally designed pages of instructions for teaching all lessons in *The Story of Hope*.
- **The Story of Hope ESL Leader's Guide** contains 83 professionally designed pages of instructions for using the Global English Edition of *The Story of Hope* in teaching English as a second language.
- Free downloadable leader's guide and ESL guide available at www.GoodSoil.com/Free

Class Facilitator's Guide
For Teaching *The Story of Hope* in 31 Class Sessions

FREE curriculum and instruction guide for facilitating a class through The Story of Hope in 31 engaging, interactive and FUN class sessions.

The Story of Hope Kids Edition

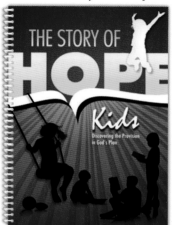

Discovering the Provision in God's Plan

This edition is visually designed and language-level adapted for kids, ages 8-12. It contains the same core content as the adult-level version of *The Story of Hope*, including the 40 Bible-event lessons, Chronological Bridge to Life, and Bible maps.

The Story of Hope–Condensed

This pocket-sized version of *The Story of Hope* includes full color images of 20 Bible events in a condensed story. Corresponding Scripture verses are included with each event. Its convenient size allows you to carry this booklet in your pocket, keep it in your car or purse. The 20 events highlight key points in the Bible's redemptive story, from beginning to end.

Mobile Apps
Available on Apple Store and Google Play

Search for *"The Story of Hope"* and/or *"The Roots of Faith"* to be able to "swipe" your way through 20, 40, and 100 beautifully visualized Bible events. Trace the Bible's story of redemption as it is woven from Genesis through Revelation. Easily share God's truth right from your mobile device!

The Way to Joy

The Way to Joy is a leader-guided foundational Bible study book, intended primarily for use as a follow-up discipleship study. Its primary use is for one-on-one sessions. However, it can also be used in small groups or as a study book for new converts' classes.

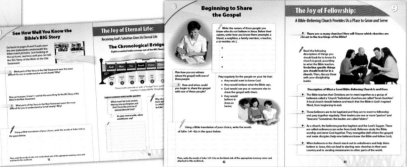

The Way to Joy Kids Edition

This book is a study in basic discipleship for kids, ages 8-12. It's a visual-design and language-level adapted version of *The Way to Joy* for adults. Most of the content is essentially the same as the adult version of *The Way to Joy*, but some content has been adapted (and added) for the needs of kids.

Free Leader's Guides Available

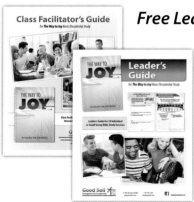

- *The Way to Joy Leader's Guide* contains 44 pages of instructions for leading a foundational discipleship study with individuals or small groups, using *The Way to Joy*.

- *The Way to Joy Class Facilitator's Guide* contains 42 pages of instructions and teaching resources for facilitating an interactive group study in a classroom setting, using *The Way to Joy*.

- Free downloadable leader's guide and class facilitator guide available at www.GoodSoil.com/Free

For Presenting the Redemptive Story with Visual Impact
Printed and Laminated Teaching Visuals (Double-sided 13.5" x 10.75")

The Bible's Big Story Teaching Visuals
Set of 100 (plus 5) teaching visuals

- 50 Old Testament event visuals
- 50 New Testament event visuals
- 5 Muslim-ministry specific visuals
- Bible event images on front
- Key teaching content on back
- Teaching content can be internationalized

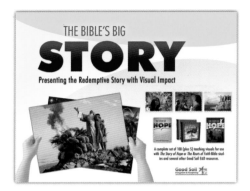

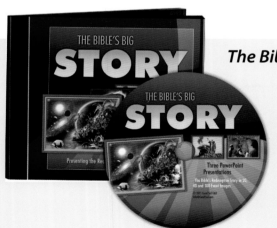

The Bible's Big Story in PowerPoint
All three presentations on one CD

Three PowerPoint presentations allow you to present the redemptive story in 20, 40 and 100 event images.

A specific presentation for The Roots of Faith courses is also included. These PowerPoint presentations contain Bible map images, the tabernacle image and the Chronological Bridge to Life. All text can be translated and changed in PowerPoint.

ChronoBridge to Life Cards

These pocket-size cards are designed to be used in presenting the Chronological Bridge to Life in personal witnessing.

The ten–card set includes an introduction card, a card for each of the eight Chronological Bridge concepts, and a Personal Response card The ten–card set includes an introduction card, a card for each of the eight Chronological Bridge concepts, and a Personal Response card.

Chronological Bridge to Life Visuals
Set of 8 teaching visuals

- Visuals for summarizing the Bible's BIG Story of redemption focusing on eight essential truths
- Includes key Bible verses and faith response statements
- Includes instructions for teaching the ChronoBridge

Hooks for Hanging the Bible's Storyline
25 Bible Eras that Summarize the Entire Bible Story

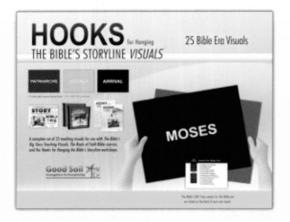

Hooks Teaching Visuals
Discovering the Provision in God's Plan

Set of 25 teaching visuals

Visuals for 25 Bible eras to use in teaching students to grasp the   Bible's storyline in as little time as two hours.

Includes one student worksheet for the Hooks—Old Testament workshop and one student worksheet for the Hooks—New Testament workshop.

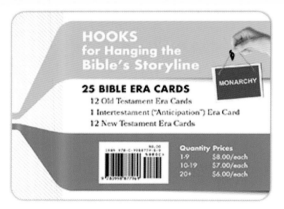

Hooks - 25 Bible Era Cards
Discovering the Provision in God's Plan

Hooks for Hanging the Bible's Storyline - pocket-size cards (4.5" x 3.375"). One card for each of 12 Old Testament eras, 12 New Testament eras, and one for the Intertestament ("Anticipation") era. Use them to learn how to think your way through the Bible, from beginning to end. Use them in facilitating Hooks for Hanging the Bible's Storyline workshops. Great for all ages. Quantity prices for 10 or more.

Chronological Bible Cards
Genesis through Revelation

A complete set of 135 pocket-size cards (4.5" x 3.375") for learning and reviewing the content and chronology of the Bible's Big Story. There is one card for each of 100 key events in 25 major Bible eras. Samples are pictured below. Plus, a bonus set of 10 Chronological Bridge to Life cards.

Chrono Bible Cards
Old Testament Events

A set of 62 pocket-size cards (4.5" x 3.375") for learning and reviewing the content and chronology of the Old Testament. There is one card for each of 50 key events in 12 major Old Testament eras.

Chrono Bible Cards
Old Testament Events

A set of 62 pocket-size cards (4.5" x 3.375") for learning and reviewing the content and chronology of the Old Testament. There is one card for each of 50 key events in 12 major Old Testament eras.

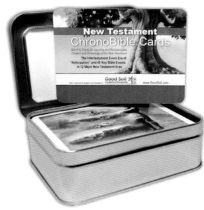

Bible Courses

Participate in *The Roots of Faith* Classes

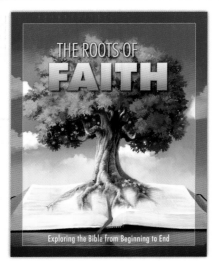

The Roots of Faith
Exploring the Bible from Beginning to End

The Roots of Faith is an extensive (100 Bible events) and intensive (80 hours of class participation) study of the Bible's redemptive story. This chronological Bible study program consists of two courses: *The Roots of Faith—Old Testament* and *The Roots of Faith—New Testament*.

In these Bible courses, you will learn …

- The basic content of the Old and New Testaments.
- The chronology of 100 major Bible events—how the Bible progressively unfolds from Genesis through Revelation.
- The geographic locations where major Bible events occurred.

Course design

- Each course (*Old Testament* and *New Testament*) consists of 40 hours of classroom instruction, Monday through Friday.
- The courses are creatively interactive and lots of fun.
- Not only will you enjoy these courses as a student, but you will also simultaneously be equipped to teach these courses. See the next page for information on *The Roots of Faith* Instructor Kits.
- Student workbooks are available for purchase by course graduates to use in teaching others.

These courses are taught in June at ABWE, near Harrisburg, PA.

www.GoodSoil.com/Roots
Training: 1.888.299.2293
Info@GoodSoil.com

The Roots of Faith
Old Testament

Unfolds the promises of the Jewish Messiah who would become the Savior of the world.

The Roots of Faith
New Testament

Unpacks the fulfillment of the Old Testament hopes and promises, based upon the perfect life and sacrificial death of Jesus Christ.

Purchase *The Roots of Faith* Instructor Kits

The Roots of Faith Instructor Kits
Curriculum for Teaching God's Redemptive Story

Two complete kits for teaching *The Roots of Faith* Bible courses, consisting of 50 lessons each.

Each kit includes:

- Workbook (50 lessons and maps)
- Set of ChronoBible cards
- Access to the online Instructor's Resource Center (IRC)
- Instructor's Guide and other needed teaching resources (videos, activities, commentary, etc.)
- Provisional certification to teach the course

www.GoodSoil.com/Resources
Orders: 1.877.959.2293

Visit Us Online

www.GoodSoil.com

The Good Soil Evangelism and Discipleship website provides:

- Information and registration links for upcoming training seminars and *The Roots of Faith* classes.
- Purchasing information and online ordering for all Good Soil resources, as well as many free downloadable resources.
- Overview of non-English translations of Good Soil resources.
- Stories of how God is using Good Soil training and resources around the world.

Visit us online at:

www.GoodSoil.com

Facebook
Good Soil Evangelism and Discipleship

"Like" us on Facebook and receive the latest updates on training events and Bible courses. Be alerted to our new Good Soil resources as they become available. Read encouraging stories of people responding in faith to the Bible's redemptive story, all over the world.

Link to the Good Soil Evangelism and Discipleship Facebook page:

www.Facebook.com/GoodSoilED/